Also by Paxton Davis

Two Soldiers
The Battle of New Market
One of the Dark Places
The Seasons of Heroes
A Flag at the Pole
Ned
Three Days

BEING A BOY

BEING

A BOY

Paxton Davis

John F. Blair, Publisher
Winston-Salem, North Carolina

Library of Congress Cataloging-in-Publication Data

Davis, Paxton, 1925-
    Being a boy/Paxton Davis.
      p.   cm.
    ISBN 0-89587-065-7
    1. Davis, Paxton, 1925-   —Biography—Youth.   2. Journalists-
-United States—Biography.   3. Winston-Salem (N.C.)—Social life and
customs.   I. Title.
PN4874.D374A3 1988
070'.92'4—dc19
[B]   88-22224
                                                          CIP

For my children
and grandchildren

and

for my sister
and hers

The author acknowledges gratefully a residential fellowship at the Virginia Center for the Creative Arts, where preparation for this book was begun.

BEING A BOY

p 141 ch 14 15
p 195 ch 19

The Orgy Begins

     Boyhood is like an orgy, a lot to do and a lot of people to do it with, and mine began on May 7, 1925, when I was hatched a few minutes before five, conveniently in time for the cocktail hour, at City Hospital, then the dominant medical institution of Winston-Salem, North Carolina. My mother, though never frail, was small; I was, it appears, vigorous; and to her surprise and everyone else's I was born two months prematurely.

At some earlier time in the twentieth century, dissatisfied with the quality of medical care available at the various small proprietary hospitals and clinics then common throughout the country, Winston-Salem's doctors and city fathers had assembled a staff and funded the erection of a public hospital that put the best medical diagnosis and equipment then known within the reach of most of the community. In those days it was widely believed that hospitals and sanatoria should be placed on high, well-aired sites to ensure optimum ventilation and sunshine; so City Hospital was built well east of downtown Winston-Salem with porches, balconies, sunrooms and sun roofs on every side of the big brick central structure. It stood at the end of the streetcar line running straight out Fourth Street, downhill and up, from Courthouse Square. It and Baptist Hospital, located across town atop a similar eminence on the hill called Ardmore, remained the city's principal hospitals for decades. City Hospital was where I and most of my contemporaries first saw light, and though it has long since been replaced, its old shell, subsequently used for a variety of public purposes, still brings a lump to my throat. Not only were my sisters and I born there but my parents were patients there at various times during my youth, and my father died there as I held his hand.

My arrival is entirely obscure to me: all I know is that my parents said, and my birth certificate confirms, that I weighed something less than five pounds, being both impatient and obstreperous. My father often embellished the data by adding that he knew me at once across the nursery because my eyes were already flashing, but all fathers say things like that. I have done so myself.

All of this is hearsay to me, however; and apart from the fact that my mother suffered from increasingly problematic varicose veins throughout her adult life, and that they were believed to be the result of "milkleg"—i.e., phlebitis—contracted during her first pregnancy, I am innocent of any mental association with the event. I remember Dr. Eugene Gray, who delivered me, but he was an intimate friend of my parents and a familiar figure of my early childhood.

My mother was confined to the hospital for more than a month afterward, I am told, while her inflammation subsided and I fattened. Then, clearly alarmed at finding herself responsible for the salvation of a small, unsanctified baby in pagan North Carolina, she and my father rushed us all to Virginia, where my maternal grandparents lived and where I was promptly, properly and conclusively christened in the beautiful eighteenth-century Fincastle Presbyterian Church in which her family had been baptized and married, and their funerals held, since the days, it sometimes seemed, of Calvin and Knox. Its brick walls, dark green shutters and elegant white columns and spire are visible beyond my window as I write, and I can almost hear, more than sixty years later, her sigh of relief at ensuring the protection of my larval soul. She came to love Winston-Salem, and for all I know may have loved it by then; but I suspect she always harbored a residual reservation about its authenticity, certainly about its gentility. Virginians are like that, especially if they are Presbyterians as well, and nothing can be done about it.

I did not know it at the time, of course, knew nothing at all, but that first passage to the putatively cooler air of Virginia initiated a pattern, in which we spent a substantial part of every summer at my grandparents' big house. It was a ritual we would follow, my mother and I, then with my sisters too, my father driving up from the baking plains of North Carolina on weekends, until my grandfather's death in 1939. Many of my baby pictures, my first steps, me playing with Granddaddy's bird dogs in the front yard with the trim picket fence beyond, were taken there, and many of my first memories are of the people there. But it is childhood in Winston-Salem I remember best.

When my first summer was over we returned to my parents' apartment on South Cherry Street in downtown Winston-Salem, but soon afterward, during the fall, we moved to the first of the two houses my parents were to own, a block apart and the focus of my life until I was grown.

Buena Vista (in Winston-Salem pronounced "Bewna" and with Vista as in "is") was the latest and the most ambitious of the neighborhoods developed around downtown as its periphery spread in every direction in the decade following World War I. Blending into West Highlands to the south and touching the small area of big houses around Forsyth Country Club to the west, it ran, on the northern end of the plateau it straddled, into the tiny, secluded enclave bordering the huge estate built by R. J. Reynolds in his last years and called by him Reynolda. Besides the mansion itself, rumored to contain a hundred rooms, Reynolda had its own golf course, greenhouses, dairy barns, blacksmith shop, post office and planned cluster of employees' cottages, all of them grouped picturesquely around a little Presbyterian church that an English village might have envied, which was the idea. But the area called "Reynolda" was larger than Reynolda proper, for the Reynolds sisters, Mrs. Kent, Mrs. Critz and Mrs. O'Hanlon, occupied with their families large houses designed by the same architect who had done Reynolda; and they stood on large, beautifully wooded lots half a mile east of the mansion where Buena Vista and Reynolda met at the intersection of Reynolda and Arbor roads.

All of that was still country in 1925, however, well west of the busy city R. J. Reynolds's initiative had created; and here and there in Buena Vista and Reynolda traces of that rural past were still visible—old barns and chicken coops yet to be pulled down in suburban backyards or empty lots of which there were many, as well as occasional rows of barbed-wire fencing where a few years earlier cows and pigs had grazed; many of the streets were still being paved, and the side streets would remain muddy until after World War II. But these were artifacts of a past R.J. Reynolds had ended: Buena Vista was new and comfortable, with the tidiest thoroughfares and handsomest houses Winston-Salem could boast in its energetic assault upon the future.

Technically Buena Vista began where its spine, Buena Vista Road, dead-ended into Reynolda Road, but few houses had been built on the long upward slope leading to the plateau; and its heart was reached only at the intersection of Buena Vista and Stratford Roads, where the Shores and Myerses occupied large houses facing each other across the trees and patchy grass of the island dividing traffic up and down the slope. But the heart of the heart began a block further west, with Oaklawn Avenue, and continued to Arbor Road, another block still. Four north-south streets crossing Buena Vista Road—Stratford, Oaklawn, Arbor and Roslyn Road—formed the main body of the neighborhood, all sweeping in perfectly straight lines to Robin Hood Road, where a huge, treeless and undeveloped area offered what we immediately named the Big Field, where, what with football and baseball, kiting and fighting, we spent much of our youth. Through its immense open space, already curbed and with sidewalks in a few places, Buena Vista's main streets, winding now, moved north a final long block to Reynolda Road, whose rows of maples, flaming in autumn, we could see in the distance.

The streets, though parallel, were far from identical. Stratford, the earliest to be developed, had once been Winston-Salem's "Lovers' Lane," and with houses on one side only, facing a dense stand of trees across the way, it retained a romantic aura.

Oaklawn was built on both sides but rolled slightly as it neared Robin Hood, while Arbor, two-sided as well, included two steep hills; and the few houses on Roslyn faced a forest to the west and had the steepest hills of all, besides which Roslyn marked, a boundary which filled small boys with awe and fear, the city limits. Across the road, deep within the piney woods through which the wind soughed so mournfully, lay, we were certain, a mysterious, possibly dangerous and certainly alluring Terra Incognita of which we spoke only in whispers. Grady Southern's theory was that it contained vast "canyons," whatever they were—and so it did, we ultimately discovered, though they proved to be big, muddy ditches of typical North Carolina erosion rather than the stony citadels we had imagined.

Our house, unoccupied before us, stood at 608 Arbor Road on the downward slope of the west side of the street, which was being paved with asphalt as we arrived. A tiny, two-story stucco house, it was hardly more than a cottage out of the Grimms: with its high gables, sparkling white walls that looked like icing on a cake and trim little front stoop, it faced Arbor from behind a giant oak tree, while the backyard became, only a few steps past the kitchen door, a dense wood where doves clustered and cooed. One of my earliest memories is of being frightened by their sound as I played in my sandbox beside the frame garage and of running inside to complain—whereupon my mother led me back, by the hand, to the sandbox, pointing to the birds in the trees and explaining why I had nothing to fear.

The house itself was anything but frightening. Besides its fairy-tale look it boasted warmth and coziness inside, with, beyond the living room stretching front to rear, a big sun porch of the sort so popular in houses of the time; and up the narrow stairs were three bedrooms with steeply sloping ceilings. Mine, scarcely larger than a closet, was at the back, overlooking the sandbox and woods, and I can still remember staring into the darkness on winter evenings and thinking, not altogether inaccurately, that we lay at the edge of an immense wilderness, perhaps like the wilderness of the Bible stories my mother read me, and that everything beyond the treetops outside my window must be undiscovered, unexplored and uninhabited. The fact that my friend Tag Montague lived three or four blocks further west, on the other side of the woods, was no more than a detail inconvenient to my small-boy's romance. It is often said that a writer's capital is in the fantasies he forms in childhood, and my fantasies of wilderness, which have surfaced again and again in my books, may well come from those early days.

Abundant black-and-white photographs confirm my infancy, for my parents, obviously enthusiastic about the box Brownie, assiduously recorded the development of their firstborn in candids carelessly, planlessly pasted to the black pages of a large green album I still have: pictures of me in my pram, round-faced, bald; sitting up against a pile of pillows in a black Windsor chair that remains in my kitchen; being fed; looking puzzled as I stand beside my grandfather, who for once in his life looks tall; in a long, fuzzy two-piece winter coverall that gives me an undeniable resemblance to a bear; kissing my first baby sister, though my expression suggests it was a performance in which I took doubtful pleasure. Usually a square black Essex, a car that vanished from the American landscape with the Depression, stands in the driveway.

But I cannot pretend that my memories from that time are quite that clear, let alone that they are coherent or consecutive: a rainbow cast by the afternoon sun across a strip of snow in the front yard; my mother nursing the same sister, an exercise I found remarkably interesting; my father coming through the door in a khaki hunting suit, then sitting on the floor and carefully disassembling and cleaning his shotgun before packing it away in its case; my great-uncle Claiborne, who was some sort of something important in New York, as handsome as a king with his white hair and red face, his dark blue city suit and derby, jolly in an armchair by the window as he told one story after another. . . . But it was still my parents' world, and until I could walk and talk and make friends of my own I would remain only a wart—a noisy, busy and growing wart, but a wart—upon its handsome countenance.

2

Origins

My parents belonged to the last generation born during the reign of Queen Victoria and like their parents and grandparents they bore the stamp. Queen Victoria and her ministers had no authority over the United States, of course, let alone over Virginia, but her influence was profound. Almost everything about my parents' youth was what we now call Victorian: clothes and manners, the stress on the importance of family and domesticity, the houses they lived in and the buildings where they worked and shopped and in which they were entertained, above all the values, often unconsciously held, by which they determined what mattered and was worth their time and moral investment. Today's stereotype of Victorianism as materialistic, humorless, rigid, sexually repressed and preoccupied with propriety is at best a partial truth. My mother's family were intensely domestic, almost obsessively concerned with their ties to one another and with the quotidian household rituals and comforts of family life, and she grew up richly nourished by the love and attention of a large circle of parents, grandparents, brothers, dogs and cats and horses and an endless array of adoring aunts and uncles; but my father's mother died so young he could hardly remember her, and his father was so improvident that his youngest son had to be brought up, haphazardly, by an older half-sister with a husband and child and obligations of her own. Far from being humorless, both families loved jokes and stories and laughter; and my parents' frequent displays of physical affection suggested lusty appetites rather than sexual anxiety and inhibition; while their prohibition of table talk about money or possessions indicated that they had little more than a modest concern for the usual symbols of material success. I think of them as flexible in their use of parental authority, too; but about the underlying things they believed in and sought to uphold—truthfulness, loyalty, unselfishness, the duty of the privileged to the less fortunate—they were severe. To that extent, at least, they conformed to the Victorian stereotype. They had standards. They took life seriously. They took themselves seriously.

In this invincible high-mindedness they were rarely solemn but typical instead of their time and class. Their sturdy, cheerful faith in the ability of reason to solve mankind's most vexing problems reflected the intellectual complacency of the late nineteenth and early twentieth centuries. They took technological success and what little they knew or understood of science as irrefutable evidence of the progress for which the world had slowly been preparing throughout modern history. Though they were Virginians directly and deeply affected by the catastrophes of war, they believed with perfect sincerity that society could alleviate suffering and poverty and salvage its dispossessed by sober thought and earnest effort; they did not excuse the racial injustice so integral to Southern life but worked to mitigate it on the assumption, which they held to the end of their lives, that in the fullness of time the Negro would be raised up, to the betterment of all. American experience of international conflict on the devastating scale of the World War, like my father's participation in it as a soldier of the American Expeditionary Force, was so brief that their innocence remained unshaken. They could not imagine a Dachau or an Auschwitz because the radical evil of totalitarianism—as opposed to global conquest, which they understood—lay outside the boundaries of their simple trust in inevitable progress, democracy and the supremacy of reason; and an atom was only the curious notion of an odd English schoolmaster. In the world of their nurturing, love, decency and justice would always triumph; there was nothing magnanimity could not—eventually—set right. Their confidence that life has meaning and purpose informed their daily lives and heavily shaped their children's.

Through his mother my father was descended from the pioneer Scotch-Irish family of Paxtons, squires and soldiers, who settled Rockbridge County, Virginia, in the early 1700s. His great-grandfather James Paxton commanded troops in the War of 1812, afterward was placed in charge of the Virginia state arsenal at Lexington, and in 1820 shot and killed a man in a duel—the details are unclear—and in consequence had to leave Lexington. He and his wife put up a large frame house on the banks of the Cowpasture River in the remote northeast corner of adjacent Botetourt County, a typical two-story white building, with front porches up and down, of what has been called the "Shenandoah Valley Federal" style. James Paxton called it, appropriately, "Soldier's Retreat." It still stands in its beautiful, secluded dell, surrounded by trees, with fine farmland rolling away in every direction. It was there that my father was born in 1886.

By then the farm's prosperity, and his family's, had vanished, and his childhood was bleak. His mother died early in his life. His father, a feckless Confederate veteran, moved her two older daughters by an earlier marriage and the four children she'd borne him to nearby Eagle Rock, where he pieced out a thin existence. Brought up by his half-sister, my father had to make do with an on-again, off-again education, and there was no money to send him, as he'd wished, to V.M.I. Instead, at sixteen, he went to Richmond and put himself through a year of business college, thereafter holding jobs at banks, insurance companies and a Roanoke store where, in 1917, he met my mother. By then, though thirty, he was still without a profession or even a substantial calling; but he had come a long way from the defeated air of Eagle Rock. He was never a joiner, but he'd become a Mason, a Shriner, and an active Presbyterian layman; above all he'd grown "citified," as they used to say, loving good clothes and wearing them so well he was always something of a dandy, enjoying the kind of food—soft-shell crabs, lobster, fine imported cheeses— unavailable in the rural scene he'd left behind. He was fond of plays and concerts and attractive women. He had not so much fled his backwater past as outgrown it, while as for work that would harness his gifts, World War I would provide that.

My mother's family were livelier and more aggressive by far, and so was she. Every generation on either side had been active in war, politics and public life. On her mother's side she was a Beckley, a great-great-granddaughter of John Beckley, first clerk of the House of Representatives, first Librarian of Congress and a founding father of the Democratic Party, and through him great-granddaughter of Alfred Beckley, a West Point graduate who commanded and surrendered a brigade of Virginia Militia in the opening months of the Civil War. Her grandfather, Alfred Beckley, was a Confederate cavalryman who'd made his way to Fincastle after Appomattox and married a local belle. But it was her father's family, the McDowells, who dominated. Like the Paxtons they were pioneer Scotch-Irish settlers; but more to the point they were energetic and effusive, intellectual and talkative, affectionate and possessive, cerebral and physical, often all at once, and all of them bursting at all times with facts, ideas, plans and a steady stream of opinions to whose conformity with prevailing sentiment they were blithely indifferent. Where their amiable exuberance originated was anybody's guess, but it was a family trait that appeared with exhausting regularity; and my mother was, despite her Beckley good looks, an epitomic McDowell.

Her father, Turner McDowell, was one of the most important figures of my early life and remains a vivid memory. Though physically unprepossessing, he had an authority of manner to which almost everyone deferred: he had intellect and judgment alike, to which he added competence, and other men sensibly sought out his counsel and liked to test their notions against his. He had what Henry Adams called in

Rooney Lee "the habit of command," a trait common to Virginians of his era and class; and it won him widespread respect within Democratic circles, in the post–Civil War South dominated by a succession of "machines" that were nothing, at bottom, but continuous oligarchies of the well-born.

My mother, born in 1893, was his first child and only daughter. They named her Emily Beckley McDowell in honor of a great-grandmother, which proved to be perceptive, for she strongly resembled the Beckleys, with a pretty, clean-cut face and tiny, delicate frame; but there was nothing delicate about her mind or personality, and almost from the first she revealed herself to be quintessentially a McDowell. As a child, if reports are to be credited, she added a sturdy disposition to question and argue to a marked intellectual capacity; and though intensely feminine she showed little willingness to play a passive "woman's" role in any of her undertakings. This was unlike her mother, who appeared to accede calmly to the prevailing Victorian view of the proper place of women; but it reflected perfectly the McDowells, who were never calm, challenged everything and instinctively viewed women as in every respect—except, perhaps, the roughneck sports at which so many of them excelled—the equals of men. Thus my mother's intelligence was encouraged, her questions taken seriously, her opinions sought and respected.

Like Virginia Woolf she was given the run of her father's fine library, so that her knowledge of history and English literature began to accumulate in early life.

She went on in 1911 to Converse College, a young, degree-granting institution—then still a novelty in women's education—in Spartanburg, South Carolina, from which she graduated in 1915 as valedictorian; and after a year teaching in Fincastle, where she handled Latin, English and math, she took a second teaching job at St. Hilda's Hall in Charles Town, West Virginia, returning in 1918 to Converse as a junior faculty member and graduate student. Her M.A. in English followed—her thesis was on "The Diction and Style of O. Henry," then highly regarded—and that was to cement an academic relationship that lasted until her death. She was successively undergraduate, graduate student and faculty member, chairman of the drive to build a modern library, president of the alumnae association and finally member of the board of trustees. For more than forty years she gave Converse her passionate loyalty.

My parents met about the time the United States entered World War I, when my mother and grandmother came into the Roanoke store where my father was working. They were shopping for phonograph records, but that task was soon forgotten as my grandmother began to "place" him, as Virginians do, and the inevitable attractions had been felt. Afterward it seemed to them both foreordained. By then thirty, he must have had numerous romantic attachments, while the list of her suitors—one of whom, promptly dismissed, had sent her an engagement ring in a cake—was said to have been long. But neither looked elsewhere again.

Their engagement proved to be long as well. My mother was already committed to St. Hilda's, and my grandparents may have insisted on time. A more compelling reason, however, was that my father soon entered the U.S. Army and expected to be sent to France. He was inducted into the coast artillery, then into one of its trench mortar battalions; but first he was sent for several months to the University of Virginia and a special school there where he was introduced to the newly acquired trucks with which the army was modernizing its system of transport, and it was as a fledgling truck "expert" that—after contracting flu and being hospitalized on a ship in the Delaware River—he joined the American Expeditionary Force overseas. He landed at Brest and started down the gangplank of the *Aquitania*, rifle and full field pack on his back, when suddenly steam whistles began to sound and bands to play. It was 11 a.m. November 11, 1918, the moment at which the long-sought Armistice that ended the war took effect; ever after he loved to tell how Kaiser Wilhelm had thrown in the towel at the news of his arrival.

He was not home again until the spring of 1919, while my mother was teaching and working on her master's at Converse; he fumed at having to be closely chaperoned at every moment they were together. But his prospects had greatly brightened thanks to the army. As a truck man in a society that knew little about trucks, he found his knowledge in demand. He worked briefly for Buick in Roanoke, then was sought out by Packard, which sent him to a comprehensive truck program in Detroit. When he finished his expertise was established. The Reynolds Tobacco Company in Winston-Salem heard of him from Packard and offered him a pioneering job heading its transport and storage division and converting it from its traditional horse-drawn drays to modern automotive transportation. He joined the company in the fall of 1920 and remained there for the rest of his life.

They were married at last on June 22, 1921—the longest day of the year, my father joked—in the Fincastle Presbyterian Church, and after a honeymoon at Mountain Lake, Virginia, moved to rooms in Winston-Salem. Few husbands and wives were ever better suited to each other, I think. Both were attractive and stylish, so that they were striking to look at; but their compatibility went far deeper. Though hardly slow—it was often said, in fact, that he moved like a dancer or boxer—my father was deliberate and exact in whatever he did, from packing a suitcase to writing a report, and this reflected the extraordinary serenity at the center of his personality: he was never solemn, had twinkling blue eyes and an air of silent amusement, but he bore himself with the unhurried manner the Romans called *gravitas*, the weight of judgment; and others learned to respect the disinterested balance with which his judgment worked. His almost unshakable calmness also made him especially gentle, and that made his company soothing and unthreatening.

My mother's judgment was usually excellent too, but she seldom reached it calmly. Her mind, so well-stocked by upbringing and education, was in perpetual ferment, for she had sharp intuitions as well and could see a thousand sides to every question, meanwhile forming an opinion about each; and to the vigorous activity of her intelligence she added a fierce zeal for the betterment of the human condition. Her belief in brotherhood provoked in her an angry passion for justice: she despised what she regarded as unfair or unjust, whether it was personal or societal, and this led her to outspoken championship of a variety of liberal causes—feminism, the League of Nations and especially the repudiation of racism. But her fervor and energy, when added to the rapidity with which she saw and mastered important points, made her impatient, not only with those she viewed as reactionaries but with people simply slower or less committed than she; she did not suffer fools gladly, nor dullards nor laggards nor the mentally lazy.

They handsomely complemented one another, my mother's strong conviction and sense of mission stirring my father's tendency to complacency if not indifference toward the world beyond his immediate ken, his reflexive patience and good sense balancing her tendency to find extremes, absolutes and villains. Both recognized too the benign polarity and resulting harmony of their natures and depended upon it for constant correction, each counting on the other for stimulation and stability.

They were aristocrats, knew it and would not have dreamed of apologizing for it. In a more egalitarian time that believes itself liberated from class-consciousness, this may need explanation. They were not snobs: though both took abundant pride in blood and lineage, like many Virginians before and after them, they were bedrock democrats and Democrats who respected merit and quality and those who had risen because of them. Serene or intense, moderate or immoderate though each might be in the particulars of personality, they shared the aristocratic conviction that fortunate birth imposed upon them special obligations to the society they lived in, believed they had a duty to lead and elevate by setting an example of disinterested public spirit. Those who snicker at the presumed arrogance of *noblesse oblige* overlook the hard truth that civilization requires leaders and throughout its history has mostly had to draw them from its upper classes. My parents had nothing but contempt for money-grubbing, the vulgarities of the *nouveaux riches* or the abuse of privilege, but—also despising cant—they knew that they'd been born to privilege themselves; and thus they determined that they owed the world exemplary lives in return. This may have been naive, but it was not hypocritical. It expressed perfectly a kind of Victorian Brahminism, once familiar in American life, that has all but vanished in later, indulged and indulgent generations. Demanding standards of service and self-denial, of "high thinking and plain living," were its hallmark, and my parents'. They belonged to an old moral tradition, especially prominent in New England and Virginia, that seems to have died in the decades since they did. In their time they seemed worldly; in ours they would seem innocent. They could be wrong, of course, and sometimes were; they could make mistakes and sometimes did. But their errors and shortcomings were due to faults of perception and appreciation, not to pettiness or vindictiveness, and their magnanimity was unfailing. They had a code and were faithful to it; their conception of duty was broad and generous. They understood honor; I do not think they would have understood fear of Russia, Watergate, sexual explicitness, thermonuclear war or the domination of public life by the sleazy, the simple-minded and the second-rate. Fortunately or unfortunately, they did not live long enough to have to try.

3

By Salem Creek

Winston-Salem to which my father brought his bride in 1921, was in the 1920s and early 1930s a small industrial city of 40,000 in the pleasantly rolling tobacco country bordering the foothills of northwestern North Carolina. Salem, by nearly a century the older part of town, had been founded in the 1760s by Moravians, a Protestant church, who, working southward from their initial American settlements in Pennsylvania, established hardy and enduring communities in the Yadkin River valley of North Carolina on a large tract they called Wachovia, founding not only Salem, which became the headquarters of their southern province, but Bethabara and Bethania, nearby villages of similar, typical neatness, prettiness and order. The Moravians were German and pious, with a way of life that revolved around the church and its customs; but they were also industrious and efficient, good artisans, merchants and planners, and their flourishing, substantial small town set a special cultural stamp—with their passion for music, their sturdy but handsome public and private buildings and their appetite for the pleasures of domesticity—on what was to become Winston-Salem. (Today "Old Salem," beautifully restored and maintained, is, like the far more pretentious Colonial Williamsburg, one of the most successful evocations of eighteenth-century America.) They gave it its unusual ambience combining worldliness and spirituality, for though Moravians can claim a Reformation history antedating Martin Luther's by decades, they are the least fanatical, most tolerant of denominations; they profess subjection to Biblical authority but value the grace of good Christian lives above adherence to creed. Theirs is a church of great sweetness and warmth, and this too has proved a crucial element in the evolution of Winston-Salem's amenity and urbanity.

Salem was Moravian, old and quiet, but we were Presbyterian and lived in the younger and far livelier part of the

city, which was Winston. My parents were Virginians, thus in
North Carolina as exotic as Hottentots, and newcomers to
boot, having come south together only after their marriage.
They were part of the tobacco world as well, for my father
was head of a department of the R. J. Reynolds Tobacco
Company, which was at the heart—which *was* the heart—of
the city's notable prosperity, and in its vitality symbolized it
too. Tobacco had built Winston, a village a mile or two north
of Salem that began suddenly to bustle and swell after the
development of plug and eventually cigarette machine-man-
ufacturing in the middle of the nineteenth century. Scores of
small factories lined the business streets by the 1880s, as well
as warehouses where leaf was marketed at auction in the fall;
but that busy diversity ended in the latter decade of the century when the Dukes, of Durham, began to merge them with
great ruthlessness into a single industrial monopoly that Buck
Duke called the American Tobacco Company. The United
States Supreme Court called it a trust, however, and ordered
its dispersion; whereupon R. J. Reynolds, another Virginian
who a few years earlier had watched with dismay as his factory was swallowed up by Duke, exuberantly seized his
opportunity and took back his company. His invention of
Camel cigarettes and Prince Albert pipe tobacco, plus his
inspired decision to concentrate both production and advertising on them, soon made his the largest and most profitable

tobacco company in the world and him one of America's
wealthiest men.

The Reynolds legend pervaded Winston life, the legend of
a swashbuckling post-bellum redneck who'd whipped Buck
Duke at his own game, and the Reynolds presence was visible
everywhere: in the twenty-two story Reynolds Building, in
1931 North Carolina's tallest, standing at the center of town;
in the long maroon trucks hauling hogsheads of leaf from
warehouse to factory; above all in the acre upon acre of factories themselves, a long wave of red brick undulating across
East Winston cheek-by-jowl with the numberless shanties
where the black Reynolds laborers lived. Winston smelled
pleasantly of tobacco most of the time and some said it
smelled of money too; and the Reynolds legend extended to
the Wachovia Bank and Trust Company, which stood sym-
bolically, symbiotically across Courthouse Square from the
Reynolds skyscraper, to which it unarguably owed its own
prosperity. A cognate legend was that of Winston's hundred
or so "reluctant millionaires," the company clerks, book-
keepers and foremen whom R. J. Reynolds wheedled and
bullied, in earlier days, to buy stock in his daring enterprise
on money borrowed from Wachovia and secured by mort-
gages, fear and the stock itself; he'd made them rich thus,
and his own family too, though unlike him and the rest of
the Reynoldses, who lived like rajahs and loved the fleshly

pleasures money brought, the Reluctants continued to huddle within their modest cottages in West End and Ardmore, still unconvinced of the reality or permanence of the fortunes Reynolds and his high-handed self-confidence had forced on them. Everyone knew who they were, for, still wearing their green eyeshades and perched on their high stools, they perfectly represented how dramatic had been the impact of tobacco and R. J. Reynolds on the tiny county seat Winston had been until their arrival.

"Mr. R. J."— "Mr. Dick" to some—was only a vivid memory by my time, even by the time my parents moved to town, for he'd died, still in his lusty prime, in 1918; but his less flamboyant younger brother, W. N. Reynolds, whom everyone called "Mr. Will," maintained tight control of the company and whatever important went on in the community. Meanwhile, however—none of R. J. Reynolds's children proving interested and W. N. Reynolds being childless—a new generation of entrepreneurs, money men and managers were assuming local positions of power: Bowman and James A. Gray, sons of the Wachovia Bank boss who'd footed the rise of Dick Reynolds and grown rich in the process, now crossed the square to take up the top levels at Reynolds, second only to "Mr. Will"; and the various sons of the various branches of the large Hanes family, Huber and Jim, Bob and Ralph, whose forebears had been prudent enough to switch from tobacco to textiles, to manufacturing underwear, socks and ladies' hose, in turn ran whatever the Reynoldses and Grays did not. They were the city's patriarchs, autocratic and unapologetic about it, and few aspects of Winston business or social and cultural life escaped their indelicate mastery; but they were benevolent unless challenged, and their foresight, ability and energy, not to mention their philanthropic generosity, made their demesne one of the New South's fairest. The Moravian grandees were tough too but stood somewhat apart, though mostly on friendly terms, and in this they had little choice: by 1910 Winston had pushed its reach north, south, east and west, its population growing as dynamically as Salem's was slumbering, and in 1913 the reality that the new had wholly surrounded the old, if not swallowed it, received legal recognition when they were merged into the single, hyphenated city of Winston-Salem. In North Carolina only Charlotte, a hundred miles south, was larger; and Winston-Salem regarded Charlotte as an overgrown milltown.

It was nothing of the sort, of course, but then, whatever self-doubt the criticism implied, neither was Winston-Salem. No one familiar with the twentieth-century South needs to be reminded how cruelly modern industry has tarnished the beauty of the landscape. It has brought jobs for many, wealth for a few, and it has meant widespread progress, if not prosperity, for a society left destitute by the Civil War the South thoroughly lost; but it has resulted as well in milltowns, especially where textiles were dominant, in whole counties of surpassing ugliness and squalor, in vile plants and viler rows of the rotting pine clapboard shacks (rented from the factory owners) of the work force. Many of the factories are closed now, many of the milltowns have since World War II been abandoned or improved, but the scars of red-clay erosion and marginal lives for white and black alike have never really healed.

Winston-Salem was not like that, either in appearance or spirit. It had its black shanties, like most Southern communities then and now, and what they revealed about the racial complacency of the local oligarchs cast honor on none of them; but the generally comfortable circumstances in which its citizens lived was reflected in a cityscape that gave immense satisfaction to the eye and a way of life elevated well above the hillbilly banality in which most Southern cities were content to dwell.

The reasons were mixed. One was the Moravians, who had brought a substantial culture to the Colonies and then preserved it doggedly; besides their abiding affection for music—their brass choirs and choral singing, their original and beautiful music from Germany and the age of Bach, their integration of their chorales with every event of the church or secular calendar—they were meticulous educators and historiographers, creating in Salem Academy and College the first institution for the higher education of women in the United States, maintaining within their sturdy archives not only their music but the most detailed records of any early American community; and their architecture, though unpretentious, could boast great charm, with its fanlights, deep-set windows, brick facades born of North Carolina's red clay and their unusual doorstep hoods, cantilevered and bent in a handsome curve that gave their houses and churches a striking and unmistakable distinction.

To the influence of the Moravians was added the mild tenor of North Carolina itself, which—though Jonathan Daniels called it "a vale of humility between two mountains of conceit"—had the advantage over Virginia and South Carolina of a modest yeomen's history and a consequent tendency toward tolerance and progress rather than bigotry and self-destructive nostalgia. North Carolina had lost more men than any other Confederate state at Gettysburg, and her sons had held a high Rebel reputation for hardiness and valor; but once Appomattox was a fact they'd returned to plow and village looking forward to better times. Besides, North Carolina had escaped the worst ravages of the fighting. The Old North State, as it styled itself, had an eye for industry as well, and in the University of North Carolina, at Chapel Hill, it could claim the first of America's state universities and, at a time when shabby mediocrity was characteristic of most Southern colleges, not only one of the country's best but the only state university below the Mason-Dixon line with a national reputation. It was a reputation, moreover, for social and political enlightenment, with Rupert Vance, Howard Odum and Frank Graham leading the way.

A third element, perhaps conclusive, may also have been fortuitous. Perhaps by design but more likely by luck, the Moravians settling Wachovia placed their headquarters in a location that happily wed a comfortable geography and a temperate climate; and this turned out, nearly a century later, to be the hub also of the primitive roads by then cobwebbing Forsyth County, hence an ideal site for their county seat and courthouse, which they proposed to call Winston. Their choice proved to be good in more respects than its centrality. Clean and abundant water was available from the many streams flowing toward the Yadkin; the ground was high enough to be reasonably dry but also not too high to be reasonably warm for most of the year; and as Winston grew and spread, the natural disposition of the several hills around downtown provided not only ample room for expansion but a pleasing separation of the developing city into neighborhoods that gave it diversity but did not violate its essential unity.

No doubt this was chance, but it was a fortunate chance, for it encouraged good humor, good will and an optimistic cast of mind. It was also the sort of fortunate chance that makes one place beautiful and livable and the next dreary and only barely habitable. Winston's Courthouse Square, the focal point of its industrial and business community, occupied the top of one plateau, with a fine flat area stretching westward a mile or so, and that became "downtown" and the early residential district too. A sharp slope east, past the Reynolds factories and the black district, led up to another hilltop of small working-class houses; while a gentler slope fell away south to Salem Creek, along and above the reaches of which lay Salem itself. To the hillside rising south of the creek early developers migrated. Then, as the western streets of the downtown plateau filled, new streets were laid out and houses built up and across the enormous hill to the southwest, and something similar took place about the same time to the smaller westerly slope nearby; and a large residential neighborhood, working-class becoming middle-class as the distance from downtown grew, appeared along the major road leading north. Finally, in the mid-1920s, a development of large lots that sold for high prices was opened two miles northwest, where until then small farms and pine forests had straddled still another hilltop. Creeks and valleys lay between each of these neighborhoods, however, and each was to assume its particular look and identity. It was in one of them that I grew up.

4

Deepening in Sin

One bright fall morning in 1927 my father led me out onto one of the sun decks at City Hospital, lifted me to his shoulders and pointed to an airplane flying overhead.

"Take a good look," he said. "It's the *Spirit of St. Louis* and Lindbergh's flying it."

By then I must have known who Lindbergh and his legendary monoplane were, for they had won the affection of the world that spring; but for years I wondered privately, telling no one for fear my doubts would be confirmed, if my memory of them might not be, in fact, the romantic invention of a busy young mind. Then in 1949, by that time a reporter for the *Winston-Salem Journal*, I finally summoned the courage to find out once and for all. To my great relief the newspaper's microfilm files bore out my memory: Lindbergh had indeed flown into town, and over the hospital, in early October 1927 while making his barnstorming tour of the United States, glamorously promoting aviation on his return from his triumphant flight to Paris.

I remember the occasion for an additional reason, how-ever: the first of my two younger sisters had just been born, and my father and I had gone to the hospital to see her and my mother. Perhaps the Freudians are correct when they assure us that the birth of a sibling is a traumatic event, especially for a first child who until then has claimed the exclusive love and attention of its parents; but I remember nothing of the sort. My baby sister Anne McDowell was small, wrinkled and above all a girl, and I could no more regard her as a rival than I could imagine transatlantic flight. I remember mainly that I was supposed to protect her.

I was four months past two at that point and already vig-orously involved in the world of Arbor Road. Besides my sandbox out back where the doves cooed in the trees I had a friend of sorts next door, a red-headed, freckle-faced giant of a boy a year or two older named Ralph, as well as a girl friend another door down beyond Ralph's; her name was Johnny Bennett, and though she too was slightly older than I she became my first real crony, companion of a hundred adventures on the sidewalks and in the bosky backyards and mysterious recesses of the neighborhood's garages. A third early friend, sometimes on, often off, was Tag Montague, who lived three blocks west across the woods in a big house standing all alone against the forest wall that seemed to mark the end of civilization; he was the first of us all to be allowed to go downtown by himself, a privilege promising such exotic pleasures it was difficult for me to ask to do so too. His father, with whom he and I were sometimes permitted to lunch, was a famous hero of the World War, a dashing man with a mustache whose pursuit plane had been downed by the Huns and who'd come home from his German prison to be decorated and celebrated. My father—who did not, after all, have a mustache or the panache of a pilot—thought him a show-off; but I did not know that until I was grown and had reached the same conclusion.

Meanwhile, Anne grew. Like me she had dark hair and fair skin, but her blue eyes were heavily lashed and deeply set, so that at all times she seemed to regard the world with a steely look from some hidden inner chamber of wisdom and judgment, whereas my eyes, though equally blue, were round and instantly readable, leaving me perfectly and permanently self-revealing. Heredity often takes curious turns, as Sherlock

Holmes observed to the worshipful Watson, and it did with us: though named for my father and always like him physically, I had my mother's restless, questioning, and impatient nature, while Anne, though looking like a Beckley, was blessed with our father's serene detachment, as if she accepted life as she found it but had little interest in correcting its many obvious flaws. She resembled him too in that she was a restful child to bring up or be with, patient, trusting, easy to please and slow to anger, though from the first she exhibited a granitic stubbornness—again like Daddy's—that made her difficult to budge from whatever position she'd carefully reached; and her anger, once fired, could be awesome. I was like Mother, volatile and with a quick temper, though I also cooled down promptly and rarely held a grudge. Anne and Daddy held few either, but they could be unyielding once hurt.

She was pretty and happy as well as calm, but to my surprise she proved quite good at roughhousing, which was my second nature and which I considered my prerogative. Her ability to hold her own seemed to me transparently unfair, but our parents cheered her on. Now and then, of course, she came a cropper. Christmas Eve 1928 we were all on the sun porch trimming the tree when the doorbell rang. My parents went to answer it—a friend bringing presents—and as they talked in the living room I watched in horror as Anne reached out from her highchair, removed a large blue ball from the nearest branch and calmly proceeded to eat it. I can still see the lines of blood coursing from her lips. I shrieked, my parents came running and Mother tore off again, this time to the kitchen, emerging an instant later with a saucepan from which she ladled spoon after spoon of steaming oatmeal into my sister's mouth. Her quick wit saved the day. Anne escaped unhurt, never even deigning to cry at the pain. Such was her stoicism.

We were together much of the time, inevitably, but during her first two or three years she seldom got beyond the yard without the maid or a parent. By then I was allowed the run of the neighborhood, at least on our side of the street. For a while Ralph was a regular playmate, for I was fascinated by his gift for trouble; but our friendship ended one summer afternoon when my father brought home from work a special present—a model of Pierce-Arrow's fanciest fire truck. It remains in my memory the most elegant toy of my childhood: perhaps as much as a yard long, sturdily built of steel and with intricate bells, ladders, swivels, pulleys and decorations. But Ralph, no doubt jealous, decided I was not to enjoy it. We were playing with it in the driveway. He ducked off home but was back in a moment with a hammer with which he proceeded, saying not a word, to smash my fire truck to bits. By the time the noise brought my parents out the destruction was complete. I had never seen my father angry, and I never saw him that angry again, but he almost turned black. It proved to be the last time I played with Ralph, and soon—though I do not claim the one was the consequence of the other—his family left Arbor Road for a different part of town. Years later our paths crossed in high school, but he did not even remember me. I assume he ended on the gallows.

On occasion, when invited, I spent the day at Tag's, trudging anxiously through the woods to his lonely house, and we poked around the nooks and crannies there; but the much greater part of my time was spent with Johnny. She was blonde, sassy and as adventurous as I, and from the first I loved her painfully, once daring to kiss her in Miss Terrell Young's nursery at the First Presbyterian Church Sunday School and dashing home afterward to deliver the exciting news to Mother. Most of our forays were less dramatic and wholly unromantic, however. We played in my sandbox and hers. We played tag in her front yard. We took lunch and had naps together. We ate Milky Ways provided by her big brother Bert, "Boy B," whom I worshiped doggedly. At four or five we stole off into the woods behind my house, pulled down our underpants and examined one another with intense—and intensely innocent—curiosity, much amused by what we found. One day when we were standing in her driveway a huge zeppelin flew directly overhead, so low and so quiet we could hear its passengers talking in the gondola.

I had little sense of time, like most small children, and remember those Arbor Road days as if all of them happened simultaneously. One spring morning Daddy brought home a young black woman from South Carolina named Emma Mozon, who stepped across the kitchen floor to pick up Anne, still crawling: she stayed with us until we were grown—cook, nurse, laundress, cleaning woman, alternative mother and intimate friend, creator of a thousand delicacies whose ingredients she invariably meted out by eye and thus could never pass on, source of infinite human wisdom and the person to whom Anne and I instinctively turned when our parents died and our children were born. I do not remember whom she replaced but no one ever replaced her, either at home or in our hearts.

One afternoon while Anne was still nursing, Daddy came upstairs to tell Mother that another of her numerous McDowell uncles had come to visit but he wasn't sure which; it proved to be Jim, my grandfather's closest brother, whose looks foretold Woody Allen's and who, with the genial impracticality of his clan, had dropped in without warning from West Virginia. To compensate for his lapse, he had brought Anne and me tennis rackets, a dozen of them. Mother's uncle on the other side, Claiborne Godwin, actually the husband of her aunt Lila, came too, fine clothes, derby, hearty laugh and all; and an elderly woman named Mrs. Barnard moved next door on the uphill side and took Anne and me for exciting rides in her enormous LaSalle open touring car. A new family occupied the downhill house vacated by the infidel Lyonses and, though younger by two years, their daughter taught me to skip; her name was Helen Gordon.

I played Little Boy Blue in the Sunday School production of Mother Goose, then a frog in the spring pageant, and on both occasions nagged at Mother, in the first case to make my blue smock bluer, in the second to give my frog's suit more bumpy green warts. One of my keenest memories, confirmed by many photographs, is of my white sailor suit, which had long pants, a navy collar down the back of the blouse and blue stripes across the wrist-cuffs; it was generally grass-stained at the elbows and knees, but I had to be argued out of sleeping in it because the lanyard around the throat ended at the breast pocket in a whistle that was indecently piercing to everyone's ears but mine.

With age I deepened in sin, slowly coming to recognize it as not only my natural condition but the natural condition of a normal boyhood. When a new girl named Mary Jane Nelson appeared in the next block, a great runner and roustabout my age almost to the week, we set to work together perfecting plans and collecting matches, and one fine spring afternoon we succeeded in setting the old barn behind her house on fire; it promptly brought three firetrucks, as we'd intended, and the sounds of their sirens and bells, the roar and smell of the flames, the excitement of watching the hoses being uncoiled and the cascades of water across the roof handsomely offset the punishments, oral and otherwise, both of us caught that night, though neither of us could fathom how quickly our parents had deduced that the crime was ours. Some time after that Mary Jane's mother hauled me into an impromptu court all her own on a charge of cursing, which I stoutly but mendaciously denied; I had not picked up either the habit or my extensive vocabulary at home, in any case, and I certainly was not yet fluent enough to call a neighborhood brother and sister the "king and queen of Hell," as alleged, but I have no idea where my gift for abuse originated. That crisis had scarcely passed—or so it seems in retrospect—when, skating with Johnny, I tried to jump a curb and broke my arm instead; Dr. Lockett lived on the corner, fortunately, and put me in a cast at once, which gave me great cachet with my friends, who liked to smell at its edges as I mended. Wickedness, I discovered early, was exhilarating.

But change proceeded inexorably. School already loomed in some dismal distance, and to prepare me for its demands I was hustled off to Baptist Hospital to be circumcised and have my tonsils out beforehand, both prophylactic rituals of the era of which my principal memories are the descent of the anesthetic cone beyond Dr. Gray's face, pain at either end while I was healing, milk shakes on demand and learning to tell time, a skill my mother taught me from my first watch, the proverbial $1 Ingersoll. That rite of passage was hardly behind me when in March 1930 Mother went off to the hospital one night, and Daddy appeared at our bedsides next morning to announce with a smile that Anne and I had a new baby sister named Lila. We were still attempting to indoctrinate her in the ways of the nursery when my parents told us we were going to move.

5

A Boy's World

We did not move far. Oaklawn Avenue lay only a short block east of Arbor and parallel to it, and together they formed the north-south spine of Buena Vista; while 707 Oaklawn, which occupied the second lot from the corner— though on the opposite side of the street—thus stood hardly a block away. But we might as well have been setting forth for China. At six anything beyond immediate view seems distant, and though I could easily have seen our new house except for the trees, the trees were there and I did not.

I went with Daddy a number of times to inspect the place, and was especially taken with a large mechanical figure of a pilot at the wheel of a ship filling the dining-room window, and had to be taken back at least twice at night to see it moving while lighted; it was the promotional device of Pilot Realty, through which my parents had bought the house, and I was crushed to find it gone the day we moved. Among its numerous delights was the pipe in the pilot's mouth, which glowed on and off in time to the seesaw motion of the wheel.

We moved at last toward the end of May 1931, the excitement of new house, new street and the occasion itself proving so great I never went back inside 608 Arbor, though I have dreamed of it again and again ever since and have sought reflexively, I think, to recreate its coziness in all my own houses. My parents let me ride on the moving van, no doubt directing operations, and though I had often ridden half a block on the rear gates of the horse-drawn wagons still delivering ice and milk door-to-door, the immensity of the van almost took my breath away. When it turned on the street and backed straight up the front walk to the front door at 707 Oaklawn I was ecstatic. It was—as moving seemed—an introduction to a bright new world. Emma brought over Anne and Lila, who was still in her stroller, by sidewalk afterward; by then I was in command and ready to show them around.

The house itself looked and felt enormous, especially following the white-icing cottage Arbor Road had been. It was nothing of the sort, in fact, being a typical upper-middle-class suburban dwelling of the time, boasting four bedrooms and two baths; but it had both a living room and library, while on the opposite side of the front-to-rear center hall, which was also divided front from back, it had a big dining room with breakfast room, kitchen and walk-in pantry behind, not to mention such amenities as a large roofed side porch, which Daddy promptly made plans to screen, a concrete, two-strip driveway and a garage out back with a maid's room to one side. The maid's washroom and toilet occupied a separate unheated and uninsulated closet off the screened back porch, and how Emma survived it is a question I still cannot answer.

Except that it faced the street from around a "Dutch colonial" gable, whatever that meant, the house at 707 Oaklawn was perfectly conventional; but it was also perfectly comfortable. Mother and Daddy had the big front bedroom over the living room connected to the even bigger bedroom my sisters shared over the library; their rear wall was continuous windows, which gave the room the sunniness, since it faced east, of a morning room or sleeping porch. There was another large bedroom in front, above the dining room, and it became the guest room. I had the small back bedroom on the same side, but it was all mine and could be reached, besides, by a rear window opening onto a broad, nearly flat span of roof abutting a hickory tree next to the back porch; I was already a ferocious climber and foresaw many adventures from taking that route. The beautifully tiled bathroom between my room and the guest room was distinguished by its good size and poor water pressure, and it also had a small copper gas heater, set into the wall, to warm small bodies up quickly. The railed upstairs hall, which was like an additional room, not only connected everything on the second floor but served as Mother's office, holding her desk, typewriter and telephone—an ideal place, in short, from which she could direct the improvement of the world. For the rest, God's plenty, the lot was deep and, as was true throughout Buena Vista, deeply wooded, but with plenty of open space for children to play and parents to garden. It was typically sandy North Carolina dirt, though, eroded by its slight slant southward, and it took Daddy most of the decade, and finally many truckloads of topsoil and manure, before it accepted an even stand of bluegrass.

These charms were allure enough; but the principal attraction of Oaklawn for me was that it was a neighborhood dominated by boys, most of them my own age or near it. I had loved Arbor Road, of course, but Tag lived blocks away and the only other nearby children were Johnny and Mary Jane, who though excellent playfellows were still girls. I sensed at once that things were going to be better on Oaklawn, and indeed before much time passed the immediate neighborhood was full of contemporaries: Ozzie Young at the catercorner with Bill and Dan Williamson next door to him and Carl Holbrook and Bill McCall down the block, and, in the other direction, Wortham Wyatt and the Vaughn boys, Bobby and Stuart, Hamilton Horton and Ralph Stockton, either then or soon afterward; and only a little further, on Stratford Road, there were Perrin and Montgomery Steele, known universally as Perk and Gum, and the immortal Willie Shore, who though demonstrably the smallest boy in Buena Vista, arguably the smallest in North Carolina or even America, proved also to be the fastest ballcarrier in the endless saga of Buena Vista football. And none of that crowd included the boys who were to become my closest friends.

The first of them appeared on the front sidewalk within an hour of my arrival on the van. He was a reedy towhead who informed me at once, as if issuing a dare, that he would be six in July; since I was already six I was prepared to press the advantage of my seniority when I noticed that he was taller, thought better of it and decided to make him my best friend instead. His name was Sonny Cheek—he hated being called Fred, Jr., he said—and he lived across the street and two houses down the block. He was extremely fast on his feet and we exchanged a couple of exploratory punches that by late afternoon had developed into the first of the almost daily fistfights we had over the next five or six years. My mother and his finally concluded that we felt it our duty to fight every Saturday morning before going off cheerfully together to a cowboy movie in the afternoon. Neither of us exactly foresaw that possibility on moving day, to be sure, but the omens were good and when the sun set we were earnestly imploring each other to come over tomorrow.

We quickly found we had much in common besides being boys and loving to fight. Our first discovery—it lasted for years—was a mutual affection, bordering on mania, for playing cowboys. By then both of us had been to the movies a lot, for in the early '30s movies were plentiful, popular and cheap; and by then we'd firmly settled on westerns as our favorite screen fare, were indeed indifferent to almost everything else except, possibly, movies about the Foreign Legion. Though hardly discriminating in our tastes, we had our preferences: Sonny was partial to Buck Jones, who was tall, broad, fair, deep-voiced and deadpan, prone, as I remember him, to buckskins and closing scenes of renunciation; while I especially liked Tom Mix, the biggest cowboy star of the time, and after his decline Ken Maynard, who like Mix was dark and wore a white hat, was like Mix too in that he grinned frequently and spent much of his time onscreen performing riding tricks. Whether our tastes revealed anything about us I have no idea, but we were stubbornly faithful to them and often ended our disputes over their relative merits by pummeling each other in the afternoon dust.

Both of us already owned substantial collections of pistols, holsters and sombreros, of course, and at one point Sonny even possessed an imitation buckskin jacket, aping Buck Jones's, which the rest of us deeply envied, especially its tassels; but our chasing and shooting, while vigorous and endless, were mostly imaginary and innocent, requiring a complex knowledge of the intricacies of neighborhood backyards rather than acquaintance with the purple sage, whatever that was. There can hardly have been a shady corner of an Oaklawn Avenue garage in which one or the other did not hide, and we knew precisely how and how far to climb the abundant trees. Many were either too big or too bare of lower branches to climb successfully, but I especially, believing climbing to be my greatest talent, conceded nothing to them and invariably persuaded myself that this spring's failure would prove next fall's conquest. A visitor to the Vardells, who lived down the block, was Victor Robinson, who could climb anything, bare or branched; and he encouraged my fantasy, as did the movies' various Tarzans. Our favorite stunt, borrowed from Mix and Colonel Tim McCoy, was to drop upon one another from an accessible limb; this rarely ended in anything more impressive than scuffed hands and knees and windless middles.

Another shared passion, though we came to it when both were eight, was our electric trains. Both were Lionels, given us for Christmas, and both were in the popular, three-rail O-gauge and thus compatible. By happy chance, however, their details were different. Sonny's locomotive was a stumpy worker, mine sleek and up-to-date, and neither our cars nor accessories were identical. The result, discovered Christmas afternoon, was that when we put them together on the ping-pong table in the Cheeks' basement we could fashion a layout far more interesting than either of us could contrive separately. He had switches, I a crossing; his engine could be reversed from the transformer, mine only by stopping the train and manually working a lever in the cab. I had a station, he a barn; I had a lamppost, he a signal. Our equipment and parts were so different that a mix-up was impossible, and it is one of the curiosities of our long friendship that, fighting as much and as enthusiastically as we did, we never fought over our trains, an interest in which cooperation instead of competition was crucial. No doubt there was a lesson there, but I doubt that either of us ever even glimpsed it.

Still a third bond between Sonny and me was that we both loved to draw and loved even more to draw together. Our fathers proved resourceful in finding a steady supply of blank newsprint and shirt cardboards, and we were soon spending rainy afternoons on the floor at his house or mine busily scratching away with old pencil stubs probably purloined from Reynolds by Daddy or Mr. Cheek, who worked there too. Art did not long distract us from the satisfactions of combat, but it had its rewards, among them the realization, which must have come to us simultaneously, that we were destined one day to be as famous for our comic strips as Roy Crane, who drew "Wash Tubbs" and was my favorite, and Alex Raymond, who drew "Secret Agent X-9," would soon invent "Flash Gordon" and was Sonny's. After navy service in World War II, in fact, he studied at the Ringling School of Art in Florida, but eventually became a lawyer. I often wonder if he doodles in the margins of his yellow pads. I do.

6

The Prison Shades Descend

My parents were still driving the old square black Essex—mysteriously called by Daddy the "Noble Six"—in September 1931, so it was through its windows that I first viewed Calvin H. Wiley School. By then I must have passed it often, for it lay only a few blocks from Oaklawn, but, like a man blithely ignoring another's gallows, I did not associate it with my own carefree life. Rumors of its numerous terrors and indignities had spread through the neighborhood, however, chiefly from the Williamson brothers, who were a year or two older, and I anticipated it with the direst apprehension. It was said, for example, that W. B. Owen, the principal, punished even the meanest infractions of the rules by lashing male miscreants with a rubber hose; and forthcoming visits by Mr. Latham, Winston-Salem's superintendent of schools, were widely believed to be planned to accomplish a similar program of torture and probable dismemberment on a grander scale.

In principle I had nothing against school and, with Mother as teacher, had already discovered the pleasures of learning things; but like most boys before and after me I saw what Wordsworth called the "shades of the prison-house" closing before me and dreaded losing my freedom, which I regarded as limitless. The prospect of confinement was dreadful. In the event I need not have feared, for Mr. Owen, gentle from some crippling disability, proved the mildest and kindest of men, given at worst to stammering suggestions of improved behavior, and Mr. Latham appeared but once and then only to pat me on the head and say how much he liked my parents. But a tiny—doubtless male—reservation about institutions in general and educational institutions in particular lingered, and lingers still, as I find it has lingered with many men. American boys simply dislike authority, whether imposed by a teacher, a barber or a platoon sergeant, and are likely, given the smallest opportunity, to bellow against it as a grave violation of their most precious natural rights.

My opportunity came my first morning at Wiley, when Mother, after seeing me safely into Miss Wilson's first-grade classroom, kissed me good-bye and strode off down the hall. I waited a minute or so, making faces at Sonny and Tag across the room, then realized it was all a mistake and bolted after her. I was too late. As I rounded the corner of the building the Essex pulled away in the opposite direction. Alone and unloved, orphaned at six, I stood at the door of dreary adult life.

This Dickensian tragedy was brief. I returned to Miss Wilson's room to find a lively brawl in progress between Tag and Jack Clinard, younger son of the principal of Granville Elementary School across town. No one had missed me, or at any rate would acknowledge missing me, least of all Miss Wilson, whose hands were full separating the combatants, and I was able to resume my place without evident disgrace. Charles Delaney, Tommy Speas and Jean Stockton were busily cutting out marked colored shapes to paste onto a large marked poster. This, plus the fact that I saw the familiar faces of Mary Jane Nelson and Nancy Sue Gladstone at the next table, was promising. I settled in and boyhood resumed.

Miss Wilson, a tiny, ferrety spinster then in early middle age, was commonly called "Old Lady Wilson" behind her back, but she proved to be the most inspired and inspiring of teachers, full of energy and imagination but wonderfully patient with a child finding some new lesson difficult. We had few of them. In those days before a literal "equality" was demanded by the courts, school systems vigorously and unapologetically winnowed the quick from the dull by preschool tests and assigned them accordingly. Miss Wilson traditionally taught the brighter first-graders at Wiley, while Miss Green, the prettier but less senior young woman across the hall, got the slower. We of Miss Wilson's room were so quick, in fact, that the next year we skipped the first half of the second grade, which had the effect of putting us a semester off through high school and necessitating devious academic strategems to guarantee our graduation in June rather than January; but "skipping" halves of grades or sometimes even wholes was common practice, believed to protect good minds from boredom.

I was a good student from the first; but I can say so without immodesty only because my success was due to genes rather than diligence. Evidently I was a natural learner who absorbed and assimilated knowledge almost effortlessly, for I was reflexively lazy and made little conscious effort to do well, though throughout school and college—except for the ablative absolute and differential calculus—I almost invariably did. This has had mixed consequences: glib intellectual dilettantism on the one hand, indifferent scholarship on the other.

I did not come to Miss Wilson's classroom already reading—that distinction was held, Mother said, by my friend Jane Pollard—but I was the first to learn once there. Why I am proud of this meaningless achievement I cannot imagine.

My memories of the first grade are discontinuous, but the place, people and atmosphere are crystalline: I believe I would recognize most of my friends after nearly sixty years, and the building itself still stands and is in use, as sturdy as ever. Like its counterpart in Ardmore, it was built during the 1920s in acknowledgment of the growing westward development of Winston-Salem, but also to relieve old West End School, a huge, unbelievably ugly Victorian landmark that had served generations of Winston children. The city fathers had planned with vision, setting Wiley at one corner of a vast, mostly open area called Hanes Park, which acted both to provide city residents with abundant ball fields, tennis courts, playgrounds and a 440-yard running track, not to mention a gymnasium with indoor swimming pool, and to be an arcing green belt breaking the mounting density of dwellings and business places. Calvin H. Wiley School—named for a pioneer North Carolina educator one of whose three daughters was to teach me senior English in high school—dominated the western eminence; further still uphill, connected by a tunnel beneath intervening railroad tracks and a major city thoroughfare, lay R. J. Reynolds High School, one of the South's finest. Beside it stood Reynolds Auditorium, which was both the high school assembly place and a large public performance hall, so perfectly placed and designed that with only cosmetic refurbishing it fulfills the same purposes today. Together Hanes Park, Wiley School and Reynolds High School and Auditorium constituted a campus of which any university could have boasted.

Everything smelled of chalk and small bodies, of course, and all boys believed and warned one another that the cafeteria soup was nothing but "dishwater"; but Wiley was as nearly immaculate, the basement playrooms excepted, as human endeavor in the presence of several hundred children could make it. Classrooms above the first grade were furnished with ancient desks of oak and iron upon whose tops generations of schoolboys had carefully engraved their initials and statements of undying love, but compared to today's graffiti they were wholly clean; and each summer maintenance crews dutifully, if vainly, scoured and bleached them afresh. Inkwells were universally featured, though except in Miss Creighton's room, where she valiantly sought to impress her charges with the beauty and utility of penmanship by the Palmer Method—a mastery of spikes, loops and whirls I never achieved, though many girls did—they lay empty unless some boy of devious intentions filled his own from private stock with which to spread mischief through the school. The one of us who succeeded oftenest in those early years was Jack Clinard, whose hair and eyebrows and lashes were so fair they might have been flaxen and who seemed determined to prove that the son of a principal did not have to be either a goody-goody or a sissy. He was a boy of surpassing humor and from our first day the class clown, endlessly fecund in the invention of new pranks; but he came a cropper one morning by firing a cap pistol during the opening recitation of the Lord's Prayer. He was promptly hauled away to the cloakroom for a thrashing at the hands of little Miss Wilson, who though hardly larger than Jack had finally, son of principal though he might be, had enough. The rest of us held our breaths in admiration of his audacity and awe at his punishment, for the bellows of pain from the cloakroom suggested little less than evisceration; but presently Miss Wilson emerged with him only a step behind, and the wink he shot across the room was a triumphant vindication of his misdeed. Tommy Speas, who lived across the street from him, explained that Jack had long since grown expert at feigning agony, having been led off to the garage time and again by his father for similar crimes and misdemeanors. In a few minutes the whole affair had been forgotten.

We were a richly mixed lot, and in that diversity lay one of the great strengths of the Winston-Salem schools. Thanks to an enlightened leadership, a demanding citizenry and a local tax supplement, the system was well-financed, at least by comparison with other Southern systems, with a nine-month academic year where most of the rest were content with eight, and offering its teachers salaries that, if meagre by today's standards, were the highest in the state. But the city school board and administration had gone further. Though vigorous in placing faster students in faster classes under their ablest teachers, they were equally determined not to let social advantage unfairly favor the privileged or social disadvantage deprive the underprivileged. They believed, in the fashionable jargon of the time, in "social opportunity" that opened the doors to a better life to children of demonstrated "merit," the result being that every school noticeably represented everything from the most prosperous families of the professional and executive ranks to the poorest families from the factories. Tag's father was an official of the Wachovia Bank, for example, while Tommy's was Winston-Salem's leading ophthalmologist and Charles Delaney's was a successful practitioner; but a number of the girls in Miss Wilson's classroom, among them our brightest students with whom most of us continued all the way through high school, were from the extremely modest homes of plumbers and carpenters and factory workers seriously hurt by the Depression. Wayne Adams, a classmate invariably dressed in tattered overalls who soon became one of my best early friends, lived in Chatham Heights, a threadbare neighborhood next to the Chatham Blanket Company inhabited mostly by its assembly-line employees. At Christmas that first year of school, Mother, always an apostle of the "social gospel," drove me to his door to leave a present—a little set of tin soldiers in crimson tunics—and I can still see the bleakness of his cold cottage, utterly barren of furniture, curtains, pictures or color, wholly devoid of heat and lighted by a single, naked overhead bulb. She meant to teach me something and she did; and if the lesson is simple, even naive, I can only answer that it stuck. I blush to confess, however, that though I saw black adults all the time, at home and at my friends' as well as working the yard and on the streets and at school, I never saw black children and never thought to wonder why. Eventually Mother made me think of that too, and to realize that Winston-Salem extended its egalitarian benevolence only so far.

It was an imperfect democracy, like most, but its intentions were progressive, if limited, and within its limits it worked. When out of doors the "Chatham Heights boys" traveled in packs, perhaps self-conscious about their overalls and evident poverty; and if one happened to confront them alone, on the playground or in the boys' playroom, they could be menacing, for they knew how to fight as Sonny and I never did and were always willing to do so. I expect they thought us West Highlands and Buena Vista boys snobs and sissies, prigs freshly dressed daily and driven to and from school by mothers who must have looked to them like the women in magazines or movies. I never took any of them home, not even Wayne, and neither did my neighborhood friends; and apart from that single Christmas glimpse I never saw their houses up close. That may have been the larger truth of those years; all sorts of wounds may have resulted and remained, may linger still. But I hope otherwise. I truly liked my school friends, wherever they came from, and as a firm meliorist—though that is nowadays a liberal heresy—I continue to believe we all profited from going to school together. In the classroom we were rightly treated on equal terms, and many poorer children outshone their more privileged classmates; they clearly benefited from exposure to the best teachers and from the inevitable stimulation competition gave their latent ambitions, and many benefited, later on, in more practical ways from the good work Wiley School got from them. In turn we children of privilege learned much from them: the harsh truths of human poverty, which, if seen only at a remove, were still vivid and real; the rough give-and-take of the streets, unknown in gentler Buena Vista; the fact that quality arises not from circumstance alone but where it will; above all the chanciness of life's blessings— Wayne Adams was not poor by choice, nor I prosperous, but because sheer luck had made us so. There was another dividend. As an adult I have been struck time and again by the obvious unease and awkwardness with which friends educated more restrictively deal with those of other stations. The enforced—to be truthful, sought—homogeneity of private schools has too often left them uncomfortable anywhere else. I do not believe that would be said of any of us from Wiley.

Whatever our good fortune, we knew we belonged to common humanity. We were innocent of virtuous motive, to be sure, but democracy took.

7

Learning Mortality

We were a neighborhood of doctors, with at least a dozen within a block or two, and it was a good thing we were. In that age before sulfa drugs, antibiotics and effective vaccines, serious illness was common and death far from infrequent. A central feature of life was the vulnerability of children. Death by accident was still rare when automobiles were fewer and slower, but childhood illness was customary and often critical. Everyone knew, either at school or down the street, someone crippled by infantile paralysis. Ben Morton, a slightly older friend who lived on Buena Vista Road, was relatively lucky among polio's victims, for despite a withered arm and twisted leg, he'd regained his ability to walk; but one of the boys I knew at Camp Hanes summer after summer wore braces on both legs and could move nowhere without crutches. Polio scares closed swimming pools many years and the fear of an epidemic, confirmed by the new prominence of Franklin D. Roosevelt, its most famous victim, never vanished. Other diseases were less visible but equally sinister. At some point during the mid-1930s Sonny contracted a form of kidney disease, was bedridden for most of a year and wound up in private school, wrenched from his friends and classmates and normal academic advancement; and though he eventually recovered, his health remained so precarious throughout adolescence that he never returned to public school. Freddy Speas, three years older and one of the closest friends of my life, came down with some form of unidentified illness in his early teens and had to leave public school the same way; he too recovered and soon returned, apparently as sturdy as ever.

Respiratory infection was by far the most frequent complaint of childhood; but "chest colds" were more often critical than they are now because there were no antibiotics to discourage either their complication or spread. The inevitable result was that many ordinary head colds led to more serious ear and pulmonary infections. Mastoiditis, almost unknown today, was a familiar problem, often relieved by the surgical removal of the mastoid bone behind the ear, a dangerous operation that sometimes resulted in even more critical intracranial infection and always left the young patient with a huge crescent cavity that girls concealed with their hair but boys could only exhibit. Bronchitis was another frequent complication, with pneumonia a perennial fear; and without specific curative drugs, doctors could do almost nothing for it but put their patients to bed for long periods of time.

Everyone seemed to have his own perennial curse. An unsightly boil on one side of his nose was Grady's. Sonny had kidney infections. My sister Anne had earaches. Freddy was often sick with respiratory complaints. Regular recurrences of bronchitis were mine and remained so until, halfway through high school, they miraculously left me. The pattern became familiar. After a cold afternoon playing football on a vacant lot littered with dead leaves and dust, I'd come in sneezing. By the end of supper I'd be wheezing, and by breakfast I'd be running a fever. At that point Dr. C. A. Street, who lived in the next block, invariably put me to bed, and there I usually stayed for as long as a month. For a day or two, still closing in on being seriously ill, I found it fun to miss school, read books and draw under the warm covers; but soon the exhaustion induced by fever and the discomfort of breathing through the mucus accumulating in my chest brought the pleasure to an end. The days became dreary. I began to miss my friends, even school. Dr. Street's visits, to listen to my chest, sometimes twice daily, became monotonous, as did cough medicine. Mother's nostrum, almost a religion, was mustard plasters, which she made morning and evening by working up a witches' brew of dry mustard into a paste she then spooned out evenly between two layers of a template cut from old sheets and pillowcases, brought upstairs wrapped in steamed towels and spread, in enthusiastic anticipation of the tortures of the Gestapo, across my chest. The heat—perhaps the smell of gummy mustard, which I came to loathe—was supposed, as she said, to "draw out" the infection; and though like most home remedies it did nothing of the sort, it was harmless, gave her the satisfaction of doing something to heal me and confronted me with the dismal truth of human mortality. The application afterward of Vicks VapoRub to my inflamed skin was an additional part of the ritual, almost welcome because Vicks smelled better than mustard and cooled me as I fell asleep.

Mother was no passive victim of disease, either in her own rare or my frequent bouts of illness, and she especially gave no quarter to the prospect of intellectual vacation. This meant that once the initial euphoria had passed I was in for deep academic pressure. My school books were set out beside my bed, as well as paper and pencils. Off she went to fetch study plans from Miss Edwards or Miss Matlock or Miss

Richard. Tommy Speas brought daily assignments, greeting me sympathetically from the door—his mother was as purposeful as mine and just as ferocious. Each morning Mother took over her class of one, a grim taskmistress in the mysteries and intricacies of spelling, arithmetic, grammar and geography, in later years Latin, algebra and sentence diagrams, who believed learning never slowed; but I came, despite my feckless hatred of the discipline, to love being taught by her. Though demanding, she had rare patience when I had trouble understanding this point or that. She had a dozen ways of explaining and illustrating everything. She made me redo careless work but was quick to applaud a good lesson. She read to me tirelessly and found me wonderful books to read for myself; I remember with special delight a series of extensively illustrated histories of particular periods of English life, from which I took both a lifelong interest and a familiarity with English history greater than I can boast of with the American past. She was an incomparably gifted teacher, without rival the best of my life. Perhaps it is the measure of her powers that during the winter of my fifth grade, when I missed six weeks from bronchitis, I returned to school three weeks ahead of the class.

On the whole I was a healthy boy, however, and even managed, as the years passed, to outgrow bronchitis. Some were less fortunate. Inoculation had decreased the incidence of smallpox, diptheria, typhoid and tetanus, but childhood disease had scarcely ended and continued to take a toll. Scarlet fever was widely, deeply and rightly feared, and houses in which a child had contracted it were placed on strict public quarantine, with notices posted on their front doors. Everyone caught chicken pox, less anxiously shunned, and German measles was almost as common. No one missed red measles, including me; the green window shades, tightly drawn as a precaution against optical complications, remain a vivid reminder. Mumps went around too, puffing faces and necks, and all small boys were warned not to let it "go down," though how that was to be accomplished, or even what it meant, was not explained; I learned years later, during World War II, how it had sometimes devastated others.

But whooping cough, thanks to vaccination nowadays mostly a memory, was the worst. It afflicted many and was fatal to more than a few, and was the cause of the only tragedy to visit my family during my boyhood. I was still in the first grade and must have brought it home, whereupon Anne promptly caught it too. Both of us hacked and whooped noisily but were never seriously sick. Not so our baby sister Lila, whose lungs, at two, were still developing and made her more vulnerable. I cannot pretend to remember her well, but her bright blue eyes, round, healthy face and hair so blonde it seemed nearly white are clear, as is her merry disposition—I still see her in the kitchen with Emma and on the evening of her second birthday, shaking her head and giggling at Daddy's teasing from her high chair by the dining table.

Two weeks later she took our whooping cough and within a few days was gravely ill, her cough racking the house. Dr. Gray stayed beside her by the hour, but she soon lapsed into convulsions, and when Mother came in the morning to tell us she'd died I already knew it and to keep from crying turned away to a book with a picture of a cowboy hunting buffalo from horseback. Later Anne and I were encouraged to touch her hand in the casket in the library—a Victorian ritual intended, I suppose, to give us an early acquaintance with the inevitability of death—and found it frighteningly cold. We sat with Emma at the top of the stairs during the funeral.

8

The Clan Assembles

Lila's death was a loss from which, in some fundamental way I only began to feel when I had children of my own, my parents never wholly recovered. Years later a Winston-Salem woman, one of their friends and herself the mother of one of mine, suddenly volunteered a recollection of Daddy still vivid to her: "He was the saddest man I've ever seen," she said, "and I could do nothing to lessen his grief because I knew I'd feel exactly the same way myself." Her remark startled and troubled me, then in my teens—troubles me still, because I had and have no memory of him like that; I see him always as smiling and so happy of nature he carried everyone with him. But I suppose the truth is that he and Mother went to pains to protect Anne and me from an excess of mourning that could have damaged us permanently. They were extraordinarily quick to sense our feelings, I know now, and could often anticipate our thoughts so readily I wondered if they read our minds. But apart from Lila's death what I recall best from that year is that during it, early and late, I made the other close friends, along with Sonny, of my boyhood.

The importance of the Speas boys in my early life is impossible to exaggerate. There were five of them—at precisely three-year intervals, as they often reminded you—of whom Tommy, my contemporary and classmate from first grade through high school, was the youngest; and all possessed the remarkable vitality that can result when good minds and good looks are encouraged by circumstance and devoted parents. By the time Tommy and I met, the two older brothers, Bill and Dixon, were either out of high school or soon to be; but they were vivid presences at home, always kind to such small fry as we, and their absorption in their many interests had established a pattern of constant activity in which their younger brothers would follow—and I, their worshiping slave, would imitate. They were also, to Mother's delight and relief, boys of the finest imaginable character, not only bright, attractive and aspiring to great accomplishment but honest and honorable. They had a distinction that would have illuminated any society.

I first encountered them *en masse* one winter Saturday when Tommy had asked me down to play and have lunch. They all sat around a huge table in the breakfast room at the rear of the big frame house they occupied high above Virginia Road, six or seven blocks from Oaklawn, and, after Dr. Speas had said the blessing, the black cook brought in bowl after bowl of steaming vegetables: string beans and limas, pinto beans and stewed tomatoes, cut corn and mashed potatoes, black-eyed peas and turnip greens, all of them decked out, as taste and custom dictated, with pickles and relish, chopped onions and vinegar, hard-boiled eggs and gravy, sometimes ham and sometimes chicken and sometimes both. I suppose we had some sort of meat too, country ham or fried chicken or country steak, and the cook could always be counted on to have a pie or two, now and then a cake, to clean up on afterward. The milk flowed by the pitcher. But what I remember best about lunch at the Speases', then and on the innumerable occasions that followed down the years, was the abundance and variety of the vegetables. Mother and Emma laid on the vegetables too, but nothing like Mrs. Speas and her cook.

I expect many of the vegetables were grown by Dr. Speas himself, for he was a fervent gardener, into his old age, who weeded and mulched and pruned and picked till his nails were black; but Winston-Salem medicine did not know him that way. To his professional colleagues he was the outstanding "eye man," or ophthalmologist, in town, or even in the state, who was equally well-regarded all over the South, from every corner of which he drew the most difficult cases, for he was a pioneer in eye surgery to whom physicians referred their patients for procedures of the greatest current sophistication. In the flesh, he was thoroughly unpretentious, even unprepossessing, dark, bald, round and of only medium height, with what some mistook for gruffness but which those who knew him better knew to be a refreshing matter-of-factness that never feared the outspoken and straightforward. His eyes twinkled behind his glasses with a wry humor; and he was famous for the answer he gave an unfamiliar woman who, having missed his wife, found him hoeing out back and asked if he were Mrs. Speas's gardener. "Yes, I am," he replied, "and I get to sleep with her too."

How Mrs. Speas would have liked that I hesitate to guess. She was a woman of great purpose, angular and energetic where her husband was rotund and sly, with hair close to red and a drive to match it. She and Dr. Speas were bedrock North Carolinians in both origin and manner, direct and practical; but I've always thought her the engine of her sons' ambition, as Mother was of mine, with Dr. Speas, like Daddy, calm, deliberate and understated, serving as both model of achievement and behavior and counterweight to her tireless determination to produce perfect children. They were never intimate, our parents, but they liked and admired each other, no doubt because their lives and purposes served them as mirrors, perhaps as vehicles of correction and adjustment.

At six, in any case, I fell in love with them all, and at sixty would do it again. For all their familial similarity they were a varied lot. Bill, twelve years older, was serious and bespectacled, his features almost a replica of his mother's, already an undergraduate at Wake Forest with his sights firmly fixed on becoming a doctor. Dixon, nine years Tommy's and my senior, was slim and darkly handsome, an outstanding student and twice Eagle Scout with a passion for aviation that resulted in exquisite models and the leader's role in embedding stone markers in a hillside north of town to facilitate identification of Winston-Salem from the air—and would soon lead to a nationally coveted Boeing Scholarship to M.I.T. Charles, the middle boy, shared a birthday with me, and though six years older often shared the celebration as well, back and forth from house to house, for he was the most extroverted member of his clan, a jokester and impromptu comic who like all the Speas brothers did well at school and was interested, like Dixon, in technology; he too was dark, but more heavily built, like his father, and on occasion was given to shaking up the neighborhood with a blast from his beloved trumpet. I saw more, day to day, of Freddy and Tommy. Freddy was physically another reminder of his mother, thin and with reddish-brown hair, a boy, three years older, with an extraordinary imagination and a gift for leadership, planning and organizing; he too meant to go into medicine and was already deeply involved in chemistry and microscopy, but his additional interests included football, chess, books, crime detection and music, particularly the piano and clarinet, with the latter of which he struggled by the hour to imitate what he heard on the radio and, eventually, his idols Benny Goodman and Artie Shaw.

It amused Mother to call Tommy and me "the book ends" because we were never more than a cowlick apart in height and, with our black hair slicked to a part a razor swipe might have left, we may even, to those who saw us casually, have looked alike. While in the fifth grade at Wiley, in fact, we were cast in a school play as the twins Hip and Hop, "the standing army of Her Majesty the Queen"—though I was felled by bronchitis and had to be replaced at the last moment by another boy who read my part. But we did not resemble each other at all, similarity of height and hair apart, and though lifelong friends we were and are different in personality, interests and manner. He, like Charles and his father, was thick through trunk and hips, though never stout, where I was small-boned, narrow-chested and wiry; he must always have outweighed me and was certainly the stronger, for his preferred position was tackle and in high-school track his specialty was the shot-put. I was impulsive and lived on my imagination and nerves while he was serious, thoughtful and exact, firmly rooted, like Dr. Speas, in the real and the possible. He shared his brothers' formidable intelligence, however, and was as quick to learn and understand as he was to adopt new interests, and he shared the family's passion for music as well, playing the piano from an early age and keeping his lessons up at least through adolescence. We entered Miss Wilson's together and graduated from high school the same June night in 1942, and I cannot remember a moment when we were not close—though I strained matters when my sexual curiosity grew salacious in our early teens and he had to chide me for my "dirty mind." He came to Fort Bragg with my parents to get me when I was discharged from the Army in 1946, having left it himself only a few months before, and two years later I was a groomsman at his wedding. It was a great occasion for me, then, when midway through first grade he skated over from Virginia Road to spend the day and bring the exciting news that he and his family would soon move in to the big, empty corner house, its backyard adjoining ours, at Stratford Road and Greenbriar.

It proved to be a bumper season for friends. No one ever mistook Grady Southern for my twin, or Tommy's, for already, at seven, he was a head taller and so solidly built he probably looked years older as well. But he was shy to a fault, hiding in the moving van as it was emptied next door and darting with a look of darkest suspicion inside the house whenever I approached. His mother was his opposite in that respect, fortunately, a famous beauty who looked a lot like Vivien Leigh and was as friendly as he was skittish. She took my many questions on at once in great good humor, setting aside the chaos of moving into a new house in a new town and new state to tell me their family came from Greenville, South Carolina, that Grady was just my age and that his sister, another small beauty who shared her mother's amiability, was named Ann and was, in fact, scarcely a week apart in age from my sister Anne. All of this seemed to me excellent news but perfectly normal.

By the time the vans had left she had coaxed Grady out of hiding, though he went on eyeing me with clear foreboding, and I'd learned more. The house on the corner had been built and was owned by a Winston-Salem merchant named D. G. Craven, but he no longer lived there and was renting it out to them. Mr. Southern, who now appeared, was tall and powerfully muscled too, so that it was easy to see where Grady got his heft, and was an officer, soon to be president, of the Security Life and Trust Company, an insurance firm, still small, with its home office in Winston-Salem. It was of more interest to me, however, that—as Grady at length dropped his guard to tell me—Mr. Southern had been a star back at Furman and was a veteran of trench fighting in the Argonne Forest during the World War, and had a German helmet with a bullet hole in it as proof. Grady finally found it and brought it out to show me, whereupon I dove into our basement to fetch Daddy's doughboy helmet; we contemplated them, side by side, in delicious horror, transported together into a fantasy of glorious slaughter and heroism, and from that moment our friendship was sealed.

But his timidity, though abated, remained. He began to talk to me without bribery and even to call me by name, for a long time having to go into our backyard first, however—Daddy had had a large set of swings and bars made for Anne and me at the Reynolds shop, and finding my name difficult to remember Grady could remind himself by reading it from the steel nameplate above my swing. He soon proved to be the finest natural athlete in the neighborhood. His size and strength were accompanied by a keen eye and sharp muscular coordination, so that he was able to master any sport quickly. He was the most powerful kicker around, could punt farther and more precisely than anyone, and he could run and pass too. He was equally adroit at baseball, could pitch, cover a base or bat with the same skill; and later he showed talent for tennis and golf. Had basketball caught on in Buena Vista I have no doubt he'd have been good at it as well, for he could pivot without thinking about it and handled any sort of ball as if it were made for him. In high school and college he'd have been a star, I imagine, perhaps a major star, for he had the star player's combination of bulk, might and motor expertise; but he never showed the slightest interest in competing at that level and remained content, in complete innocence of athletic egotism or conceit, to play with his friends. He wholly lacked the killer instinct, the need to bully; and perhaps that also was an aspect of his diffidence.

Everything was now in place: Grady at one corner, Tommy and his brothers at the corner directly behind him, and I alongside Grady, with the Speases' broader backyard not only abutting his but overlapping mine, so that movement from one to another was easy, especially once we'd ripped holes in the fence where all three met. We were ready to enter the mainstream of boyhood.

9

Adventures Underground

The center of the universe now moved to the Speases' basement. This was inevitable: there were more of them, all—even Tommy by a couple of months—were older and their basement was immense. An even more persuasive reason was that Freddy was a born leader and innovator with something new to do or try every day of the week; he was not only never bored or boring but able to dispel boredom in others. He quickly became the focal figure amongst the boys at our end of Buena Vista.

He was a genius in the fine art of being a boy, but the basement helped. At a time when most American basements were still cellars—at best, like ours, partly floored with concrete but boasting only half-walls overlooking bare foundation dirt beyond—the Speases' was astonishing. The house above it was astonishing too, a vast ugly sprawl of brick with a system of roofs, porches and a porte cochère suggesting it could only have been designed in a nightmare; but its basement was its glory and redemption. Half a dozen steps down from the back drive led to a huge central open area in which Dr. Speas's rowing machine stood not far from the big hand-fed coal furnace; and around it on every side doors opened, one by one, into a series of rooms: the cook's in one corner; another beneath the sun porch, upon which we cast an eye for future disposition, with a row of ground-level windows and its own outside stair; a coal bin beneath the porte cochère and a long narrow room, filling most of one side, clearly intended, with its many deep shelves, for the storage of canned goods and odds and ends. Instead, and immediately, it became the place where the Speas boys could pursue their hobbies. Dixon had a big bench where he worked on his fabulous models, Charles another for his, and Tommy moved from one to the other as principal assistant. Freddy had a long table standing out from the interior wall upon which he or someone had built a system of shallow shelves, and it became his laboratory, littered with chemical apparatus, flasks and beakers and racks of test tubes and an alcohol lamp, at which he performed "expeerimunds," as I excitedly told Mother, now and then reaching behind him to fetch this bottle or that from the rows of chemicals aligned in perfect order. I found the colors, smells and flickering flame not only unbearably beautiful but provocative to my imagination of romantic deeds in exotic places, and vowed then and there to dedicate my life to science. I was not sure what science was, but I knew it was mysterious and dangerous, and when Freddy told me I could establish my own workplace at the end of his, no doubt in response to my nagging, Daddy dutifully made me a sturdy little table from scrap lumber and I proudly lugged it over and set it in position. Freddy told me Michael Faraday had started the same way, apprenticed to Sir Humphrey Davy, and I liked that—whoever Michael Faraday was. Whoever Sir Humphrey Davy was, for that matter.

I soon found out. Neither idleness nor ignorance was encouraged at the Speases' house or mine; encyclopedias, dictionaries, atlases and almanacs of various qualities lay everywhere, and the walls were hidden behind shelves of books of every sort: good fiction, trashy fiction, anthologies of poetry, animal tales and children's stories, history and biography, Mother's old college textbooks and student editions of *The Marble Faun* and *The Portrait of a Lady*, most of Shakespeare in the old annotated Arden edition, the Harvard Classics across one five-foot shelf, and, at the Speases', a copy of *Gray's Anat-*

omy, thumbed and soiled from Dr. Speas's student days, plus odds and ends of medical tests and handbooks over which we eagerly pored for shudders of horror. The customary response to questions of fact or record was, "Look it up!"— and we rapidly learned to, acquiring in the process not only the habit but an ungodly assemblage of memorable but mostly useless information: the death of Axel Fersen, Marie Antoinette's Swedish lover, at the hands of a mob; the operations of Gatun Lock in the Panana Canal; the lives of General Leonard B. Wood, Newton D. Baker and William G. McAdoo; the relief of Peking during the Boxer Rebellion; the curious case of Caruso's throat. Those and countless other oddments proved useful in later life, when the pursuit of trivia became an American mania, but they were of little academic value in the early 1930s. Of more immediate utility were the college textbooks in general and organic chemistry used by Bill Speas at Wake Forest through which Freddy and I wove our baffled way in search of scientific enlightenment. At eleven and eight, respectively, we understood little; but one of the books was interspersed with one-page biographical sketches, with portraits in ovals, of the great pioneering chemists, and we found them enthralling: Lavoisier and Priestley, Dalton and Davy, Faraday and Mendeleyev, Perkin and Hall, Thomson and Rutherford, not to mention the Curies and the young Englishman H.G.J. Moseley, killed at Gallipoli. Science was still cursorily taught in even the best high schools, not at all in the grammar grades; and what little we learned of it as boys, most of it probably wrong, we got from those books and from collected scientists' lives like *Crucibles* and *Microbe Hunters*, which we borrowed from libraries.

But our basement pursuits were not confined to the glorious mysteries of science. The mysteries of crime and daring deeds of dastardly criminals were the romance of American life during those pinched Depression years, and Freddy vowed to plunge us into J. Edgar Hoover's war of Tommy guns and bank stickups. The bizarre case of Leopold and Loeb had seized the public imagination only a few years before, but its psychopathology was lost on us. Instead, our notions fed by the wave of gangster movies launched noisily by the coming of sound—*Little Caesar, The Public Enemy* and *Scarface*, especially—we dreamed of pitting our brains and bravery against the mobsters and bank robbers of the Middle West whose capers had made them the Robin Hoods of contemporary newspaper folklore: Al Capone and Pretty Boy Floyd, Creepy Karpis and Baby Face Nelson, Clyde Barrow and Bonnie Parker, Machine Gun Kelly and Ma Barker, and above all John Dillinger, whose exciting exploits in and out of a place called "Little Bohemia" and seemingly happy-go-lucky personality had put him on the front page of every newspaper in the country and elevated him to the place of the FBI's "Public Enemy No. l." This was a designation that sent chills down our backs and us into every post office in town

hoping to pick up the famous wanted notice showing his fingerprints and face from front and side. Hoover himself was
our hero, for we neither understood nor cared how zealously
his self-promotion had exaggerated both the extent of crime
in America and Hoover's success in catching its perpetrators;
and when James Cagney starred in *G-Men*, an early movie
glorifying the FBI, it came as the apotheosis of our rampaging
fantasies.

Freddy, the master fantasist of us all, determined we
should play our part in Hoover's crusade; and the kidnapping
and murder of the Lindbergh baby, a sensation that dominated the news for months, only confirmed for him and us
the nation's need for our service. The result was the creation
of the Eyefindem Detective Agency, which after a day or two
became, at Freddy's direction, the Mekechum Detective
Agency, an ambitious institution through which he proposed
to organize, centralize and rationalize our efforts. Frugally, he
retained the large, heavily lashed eye on the office sign he
drew in India ink to hang above the door.

The door led, in fact, to the spare basement room beneath
the sun porch upon which Freddy had been casting apprais-
ing looks since moving in, and Dr. and Mrs. Speas obligingly
agreed to let him locate his latest project there. Though the
legendary "private eye" of Hammett and Chandler had yet to
capture public fancy, or ours, thanks to the movies we all
knew what detectives did. Post Toasties helped too by creat-

ing a radio serial built around the authoritarian figure of "Inspector Post," whose *basso profundo* pursuit of evildoers invariably ended in their arrest; and then by merchandising a corps of "Inspector Post's Detectives," in which one enlisted by sending two cereal-box tops to Battle Creek, Michigan. The system was progressive: first enrolled as a detective, one could thereafter advance in rank by passing an examination on criminology, at the rear of the detection manual, and sending in another two box tops to Post Toasties; by turns one became, assuming success at the quiz, sergeant, lieutenant and captain of detectives, each represented by a new badge, nickel-plated and with the earned rank duly stated. Freddy and his brothers had accumulated a fine collection of badges to the upper ranks, partly by diligence and partly by gorging themselves on Post Toasties; and Freddy, undertaking our one captaincy, instructed the rest of us to enroll at once. It was all very satisfactory, except that my badge arrived in the mail with the pin broken off and I fretted desperately till Daddy took it to the Reynolds shop and had it soldered back in place. I wore it everywhere.

Freddy's planning was, as usual, comprehensive. The basement room could be entered by a little concrete outside stair, but that was for clients: we detectives were directed to report and leave from the door into the basement itself, especially if, as was generally the case, on secret assignments. A panel of cup hooks held our in-and-out cards alongside the captain's desk, and each of us had a number; mine was 80 by my choice, but I no longer remember why. Freddy, a benevolent but demanding superior, was emphatic that we must turn them over immediately upon arrival and before departure. Slackness of any sort was discouraged.

His thoroughness extended to self-defense, in which he insisted we be competent. This led to a session or two of jujitsu, which few of us had ever heard of and none seen but which Freddy, who instructed us on the basis of a two-page photo spread in *American Boy*, argued was the newest thing at the FBI. We practised in undershirts, aping the pictures of Japanese experts, but mastered the holds and falls only feebly. We proved abler, like all ruffians, with firearms. Freddy had designated the space next to his desk on the inner wall as our "munitions room," and after Charles had put up nails to hold our varied weapons it was a fearsome thing to see: the neighborhood's collection of revolvers, automatics, Lugers, double-barreled shotguns and even a submachine gun fashioned for me by an older boy named Arch Taylor from a pine plank and round cheesebox dyed with black shoe wax—all toys, of course, but vivid evidence, viewed together, of boyhood's perennial fascination with guns, which I shared.

The saving feature of this fantasy of violence was that Freddy gave it shape and direction, thus limits. Once our weapons were in place on the wall we were forbidden to handle them, let alone remove them, except on his authority.

His written daily assignments not only specified what tasks we were to perform but which guns, if any, we were to use. Since most assignments dealt with such mundane duties as shadowing suspicious neighborhood characters, generally our sisters, and logging license numbers of all the cars that passed up Stratford Road between, say, lunch and sunset—a job at which Grady and I, prone in the grass behind a boxwood bush at the corner, spent many a boring afternoon—we had little need to arm ourselves; and Freddy fiercely demanded that we look "appropriate" to whatever assignment we'd been handed. The result was that, apart from ambushing Charles, who obliged us by playing Dillinger in one of Freddy's most ambitious "exercises," we did little shooting. This had the usual effect of making us dream even more yearningly of gunplay and blast-outs at "Little Bohemia"; but Freddy remained firm, and we did a lot of fingerprinting and filing, slowly coming to realize that detection was mostly dull, after all.

The humdrum routine was abruptly ended one afternoon when Mr. Sides, the postman, unexpectedly delivered a letter addressed to the Mekechum Agency. After dusting it for fingerprints and examining the envelope for further clues, Freddy carefully scrutinized the letter inside, which he'd removed with tweezers, through his magnifying glass. We all huddled at his desk to read, with a thrill, that someone—perhaps John Dillinger himself—had us under "surveillance."

The watchers were being watched and even, the note hinted, threatened—"Look out!" it ended. Freddy despatched pairs of us to the four corners of Buena Vista to keep an eye out for strangers; and when we reported back that we'd had no success the mystery deliciously deepened. This romance did not last. Just before suppertime Grady drifted in from a dentist's appointment, heard the tale and looked at the letter. "Oh, shoot," he said with a shrug. "That's just Daddy's handwriting. I heard him chuckling when he was reading it to Mother last night."

An even crueler blow fell one summer morning when I opened the paper to see a huge mug shot of Dillinger halfcovering the front page—clipped and pasted to a sheet of shirt cardboard, I thought, it would look wonderful on the agency wall. Alas for Mekechum and our valiant intentions, the news was that Dillinger was dead, gunned down by Melvin Purvis and a squad of G-men outside a Chicago movie house; and though the gunning-down was exciting, as was the mystery of the "woman in red" who'd fingered Dillinger, this was the end. Our entire fantasy had been built on his apprehension, possibly on Oaklawn Avenue, and without him detection seemed pale and pointless. Later that year Post Toasties replaced "Inspector Post" with an organizaion of "Junior G-Men" led by the redoubtable Purvis, now a national hero, with new badges and all; but by then we'd moved on to fresh adventures.

10

The Pursuit of Glory

Tommy and I were the smallest boys in the neighborhood, and knew it; but I did not know that I was also the puniest, so took to sports with manic enthusiasm. We all did, like most American boys of every generation; and in that age before televised, professionalized athletics removed every mystery from every sport, we played much of most games in our heads. Without visible models to imitate, we had to.

There were ways of learning sports, of course. I still remember my first football, roundish and with a rubber bladder that had to be inflated by mouth, and Daddy drilling me, his hat, coat and tie immaculately in place, in passing, catching and kicking in the front yard, while Mr. Southern drilled Grady, a quicker study, next door. Both of us were immensely relieved when at last they dusted off their hands, went back inside and left real football to us. Older boys handed on their knowledge and mastery almost imperceptibly, bidding smaller fry into their games as they needed them to flesh out sides. Stores selling sporting equipment often provided instructional pamphlets as well: free folders, usually illustrated with black-and-white still photographs that could be flipped to create the illusion of motion, giving lessons in the "correct" way to punt or throw a curve ball; we struggled by the hour to get just right. Every issue of such magazines as *Boys' Life, American Boy* or *Open Road for Boys* featured stories on sports and sports figures, generally offering advice guaranteeing supremacy in the skills of Red Grange, Big Bill Tilden, Bobby Jones and Babe Ruth; and every library had sports books we plundered for lore. I loved best a thick work by Pop Warner, the title of which I have forgotten, that not only told the youthful reader the rules of games and how to play them well but ways of improvising equipment: how to sew pads into the shoulders of old sweaters or the knees of corduroy knickers, how to make a tackling dummy from dry leaves and a long burlap bag of the sort we called a "towsack," the way to tape back together a split bat to make it as good as new, or almost. We used Pop Warner a lot, read the sports pages of the *Winston-Salem Journal* and *Twin City Sentinel* like scholars, followed Jimmy Foxx, Carl Hubbell, Ellsworth Vines, Eric ("the Red") Tipton and Gene Sarazen with the devotion of acolytes, hoping to learn the secrets of their stardom; and in the dark depths of the night we imagined striding to the plate, pointing to the center-field fence and pelting the first pitch over it.

Such dreams of glory were and are universal, but with us they were inevitable as well: none of us had ever seen a "real" ball game of any sort, scholastic, collegiate or professional, and until we did, which took another year or two, much of what we imagined on the diamond or gridiron was both richly romantic and hopelessly wrong. The panoply of protective equipment athletes were beginning to wear at all levels, for example, was mostly unknown to us, since our notions were based on old yearbook photographs from before the World War, when football was still played bareheaded, and shoulder, hip and kneepads, if used at all, were rudimentary and so thin they could have protected little. That was how our fathers and uncles had played, though, especially Mr. Southern, the big back at Furman, and without the close-up reality of television for correction we were perfectly satisfied to play that way too. Equipment was expensive anyway, when available, and though comfortable enough for the practical demands of daily life our parents could scarcely afford such obvious luxuries at a time of worldwide Depression. When Grady was given full football fig for Christmas one year we all shared his bounty—he may never actually have worn his helmet, in fact, a thin skullcap closer to Lindbergh's than Sid Luckman's, since I managed somehow always to have it on my head.

He never seemed to mind, though. A kind of instinctive communism was the rule, and any working football, baseball, bat or glove was viewed as common property. This was generous but it was also necessary if we were to play at all, since balls took a beating and were not easily replaced. Footballs had leather covers and laces, and those wore reasonably well; but their rubber bladders did not and often exploded from a hefty punt, which provoked great general mirth, even satisfaction, but often ended the ball game too. Baseballs came apart even more readily, as did bats—the traditional Louisville Sluggers—and without a roll of black electric tape on hand, which Freddy usually saw to, we had to call it a day then and there. Taped balls often came apart again later, and taped bats could sting the hands and wrists up to the elbows; but it was either share and tape or find something else to do. The instant replacement of the instantly obsolescent lay, with the Little League, in a more affluent future.

Another deficiency—which like many turned out to be an advantage—was that we lacked authentic playing fields. This too seemed to us unremarkable, part of the natural order of things, since the organization of athletics into systematic teams and leagues governed by rules and adults had not yet entered juvenile life, the result being that we played football and baseball in a lot of open spaces of various sizes and shapes, indifferent alike to the "official" dimensions and the technicalities of regulations we hardly understood anyway. We were clear enough about the fundamental principles, thanks to older boys and Pop Warner, but we fashioned and occasionally mangled them to suit our particular circumstances.

Football at our end of Buena Vista was reserved for the Speases' backyard, which was open, flat and—at perhaps a hundred feet—relatively long, not to mention close by to permit practise at all hours and in all weathers, which Freddy generally demanded. Other open lots dotted the neighborhood, still empty of houses, and we used them sometimes too, though they were usually uncut and rough with underbrush and ruts, even raw pine stumps, so that one could get hurt playing on them. But by far the universal favorite for baseball, kiting, fighting and football games against the West End gang was an immense spread of neat meadowland, perhaps as much as seventy or eighty acres bounded by Oaklawn Avenue and Stratford Road, that lay at the northern end of both and separated Buena Vista from Reynolda. Still undeveloped by its owner, it sloped gently this way and that but was so large, and its surface so even, that it could easily have accommodated twenty football and baseball games and left room for a circus, an airfield and the county fair. We called it "the Big Field," and throughout our decade of boyhood we probably saw more of it than we did of our own bedrooms. In the late 1930s some neighborhood philanthropist built us a backstop in the closest corner. I once fought another boy around its entire circumference. Fossilized broken bats and balls no doubt await some archaeologist of the future beneath its grassy soil, as well as the remains of countless shattered kites, skates and pop bottles. When years later I came home from World War II I went almost at once to see and touch it, our Big Field, to reassure myself that in a world mutilated and altered by destructiveness something solid remained. It was finally built over in the 1950s, but I have been able to pretend, on the whole successfully, that it is still open and serene, its bright blue sky marked only by cottony cumuli.

Our innocence of first-hand spectatorial experience did not prevent us from developing fervent loyalties. These were based on hearsay and prejudice, to be sure, but no latter-day Redskins or Cowboys fan could show greater enthusiasm. Baseball divided us by caps and the heroic images of famous players: the Speases rooted for the Giants and Red Sox, while

Grady developed what seemed to me an irrational attachment to Dizzy Dean and the Cardinals, though I—worshiping Lou Gehrig and Bill Dickey and the receding figure of Babe Ruth—could find neither authenticity nor virtue in any team but the Yankees, who to my mind represented divinity. Grady naturally followed Furman in football, the Speases Wake Forest, I the Fighting Squadron of V.M.I., and the fact that we had never seen any of them except in occasional blurred newspaper photos or for a few seconds now and then in newsreels in no way lessened our admiration. Sometimes local radio station WSJS carried a big-league game, and we usually listened; but it usually seemed pale and abstract alongside what we imagined. An exception to this isolation from the reality of sports came one sweaty summer night when, honoring my keenness for boxing, Daddy took me to the Carolina Arena in downtown Winston-Salem, where Jess Willard, by then a lumbering fat man, was refereeing wrestling. The fat fell away for an instant when he delivered what Daddy called a "rabbit punch" to an errant bozo and I saw again, or thought I saw, the young giant whose pummeling fists had toppled Jack Johnson in 1915. "Pummeling fists" was the sort of epithet I'd learned, and learned to love, from the sports pages.

Our outdoor amusements—we made no firm distinction between sports and games—followed a cycle set by the seasons. The year began with the Rose Bowl, then the only New

Year's Day game broadcast nationwide, but by that time football for us had passed with the mild fall weather. Marbles
took center stage on the Wiley School playground, played
with demonic skill by the rough boys of Chatham Heights,
who were ferocious with aggies and alleys, yaws and steelies,
cloudies and catseyes, and regularly shot ours out of the ring
and carried them off in the brown suede bags that were the
universal means of transporting one's collection; none of our
crowd played well enough to whip them, but we tried valiantly and repeatedly, begging our fathers to bring us fresh
supplies of ball bearings to replace the steelies we'd lost,
steelies being, in the early 1930s, the game's most aggressive
weapon. Presently marbles gave way to tops, nowadays all but
forgotten, which resembled wooden turnips with hard metal
points and which, if wound correctly and with enough string,
could be propelled into extraordinary spins—spins that,
taken a step further, brought them into competition with
other tops set spinning the same moment, thus creating still
another playground game. I was no better at tops than I was
at marbles, especially against the boys in overalls, and, since it
was winner take loser again, I generally was out of tops in a
few days. I fared better at yo-yos, and better still at skating
and kiting, which appropriated our energies near the end of
February. Skates in those days were made of steel and came
with a "key," actually a small wrench that adjusted the length
and toe to the skater's foot and was hung hopefully by an old

shoelace about his neck, though most were lost at once to leave their owners at the mercy of the single neighborhood skater who'd held on to his. Buena Vista had fine sidewalks throughout and should have been harmless enough, but by jumping curbs, finding the steepest hills and developing a game of street hockey using broken branches as sticks and last month's yo-yos as pucks, we succeeded in breaking a number of arms and ankles: splints, casts, slings and crutches were deeply admired and envied as badges of splendid masculinity, the terms "macho" and "machismo" having yet to be applied to small American boys pursuing such hardy pleasures as dirt and destruction.

Kiting, the game of March, was a thing of fantasy and delicacy; most of us became good, winds permitting, at launching and guiding kites until, often, they were nearly out of sight. It took just the right length of tail as well as a feel for when and how fast to let out string; and I even, with Freddy, got proficient at flying box kites, which, with their solid look and powerful tug once aloft, fascinated us both more than the traditional kites built on a single plane. We liked to send messages up the line and to design imaginary flights our kites must travel to accomplish the complex map-making missions they undertook for purposes of espionage.

The summer game, of course, for us and everyone, was baseball. We started as soon as the weather warmed and thereafter played—daily, annually, at the Big Field, at Hanes

Park, in odd lots come across accidentally, at camp, at our grandparents', on hard clay and perfect grass, when it got too hot or turned too rainy, with a dozen teammates or two, gloved or bareknuckled—till school reopened in the fall. Baseball lay so deep within us we played it reflexively, with none of the thought or planning we gave football; it was as natural as breathing, and as easy. Our rules were flexible: if the crowd was large we chose sides by going hand-to-hand up the bat for first pick, the final blow being an attempt by the loser to kick the bat from the grip of the winner, and if our teams sometimes exceeded the regulation nine that was an insignificant technicality; if the crowd was too small to make sides we played one old cat, a one-base game that left the batter at home plate until he was put out, or roll-at-the-bat, which left him there till a fielder succeeded in rolling a hit ball so it struck the bat, laid across home; and if there were only two of us we played catch or practised fielding and catching flies. We were equally casual about equipment: few could boast expensive mitts—for years mine was an old fielder's glove, handed down by my Uncle Stuart, whose pocket was so thin the ball stung like a rock if caught correctly—while balls and bats taped together after hefty wallops were the rule; anything from a towsack to a convenient bush served as a base, and we were never finicky about the slope of the field, improvising new rules and bounds as needed. What never changed was the habit: we played by whatever guidelines suited us, but from April to September our gloves hung from our handlebars, ready for such opportunity as fate chose to bring. Baseball is at the center of American boyhood's collective unconscious. We thought softball effeminate.

11

You Could Look It Up

Basketball never caught on in Buena Vista when we were boys—the first hoops and backstops began to appear over garage doors about the time of Pearl Harbor—but I doubt that I, at least, would have proved any more expert at it than I was at football or baseball. I was too small and broke too easily to become the athlete I dreamed of being; and though I persevered as energetically as if fame, a spot on Walter Camp's All-America and the love of beautiful women were my inevitable reward, I never won them. Yet if weak I was wiry, and my coordination was good enough to make me, with much practise, respectable enough at throwing, kicking, hitting and catching, so that, though no star, even in Buena Vista, I could pass a "bullet" and punt or drop-kick—in those days an exotic skill richly envied by those who lacked it—with confidence. Apart from being as squirmy as most boys, however, I was only a mediocre runner, and at blocking and tackling I usually succeeded in bruising or scuffing myself when not actually spraining an ankle or breaking my arm, collarbone or nose. I always seemed to wind up at the bottom of a pileup, my breath knocked out.

There were sports that did not require mass and power, of course, and my eventual discovery of them came with the force of a revelation. After a few false starts I emerged as a strong swimmer. When I was ten or so my uncle Stuart, the great hander-downer, gave me his old golf clubs with wooden shafts and names to revel in—niblick, mashie, midiron, spoon—unaware that already "sticks" were old hat, their names being replaced with the system of numbers, still employed today, that may be more scientific, as argued, but boasts far less romatic an aura. Every spring until I was grown I sank hollowed tin cans at either end of the backyard and fired Acushnets and Titleists back and forth at odd moments all summer on my private, carefully tended golf course. Try as I might, though, I failed to develop the overriding passion for it that golf demands. Grady and Tommy did, but that was later.

I did a lot better at tennis, which I encountered at about the same time and took to at once. Daddy had played it as a young man, and that and his ancient racquet—shaped like a snowshoe and strung too softly for the harder game of the '30s—encouraged me, though I soon had a newer racquet of my own and was committed to virtually compulsive daily play on the clay courts of Hanes Park. Tennis was still considered a game of the rich, and indeed the Forsyth Country Club, where we sometimes played, had the best courts in town; but Winston-Salem's public recreation department had built fourteen first-rate courts at Hanes Park, open to anyone, as well as others in other neighborhoods, and it maintained them beautifully. They could be reserved by telephone but that was rarely necessary; again and again Grady and I had them all to ourselves, innocent as only small boys can be to the fact that no one above the age of ten, male or female, would be foolhardy enough to stir, let alone pound a tennis ball back and forth across a court, in the baking sunlight of a North Carolina midsummer midday. In tennis as in every other sport we followed we were avid fans of the stars, at that time Fred Perry and Don Budge, Bunny Austin and Baron von Cramm, and I developed a special admiration for a Californian named Gene Mako who was Budge's perennial doubles partner; he gave me one of the great thrills of my boyhood by autographing and sending back to me a newspaper photo I'd clipped and mailed him at whatever tournament, Rye, Newport or Seabright, was in progress that week. Grady and I dreamed of becoming a legendary doubles team ourselves, another partnership of the cool precision of Bill Tilden and Vinnie Richards or Budge and Mako. In high school we got our chance at last and managed to lose every match, to the mounting consternation of Coach Walker Barnette, who told me years afterward he'd never—never anywhere, he emphasized—witnessed such incompetence. Played well or ill, and mostly the latter, tennis became one of the central pleasures of my life and remained so until I finally had to give it up in middle age; it afforded me immense satisfaction, at forty-nine, to take the first set from a good player thirty years younger.

But nothing in my long experience of sports matches being a Raven. The Ravens are little known or remembered today, in some cases even by old Ravens themselves; but in the fall of 1934—our only season, the concentration of small boys being intense but limited—we were a force to strike certain terror in the hearts of our foes: a football team, sometimes six or seven, sometimes as many as thirteen or fourteen and all playing, with such an unbroken and obviously unbreakable succession of victories that no team but our perennial weekly opponents—though we preferred to think of our rivalry as "traditional," as the sports pages put it, like Duke and Carolina, Harvard and Yale, Army and Navy—dared to challenge us. The possibility that our existence might not even be known beyond the privileged precincts of the neighborhood did not occur to us. We were, and I have every confidence we are still, the finest pigskin combination Buena Vista produced, at any rate the oddest.

Adults so thoroughly dominate children's athletics nowadays—coaching and refereeing, establishing rules and setting schedules, buying uniforms and picking lineups, above all imposing their own personalities and expectations, not to say neuroses, upon the boys and girls actually "playing" the games—that the freedom from parental interference we enjoyed half a century ago must be difficult to imagine. Whether by design or weariness or simply because they had other things to think about during hard times, our fathers and mothers left us alone to play our sports as we liked, in our own way and by our own rules and to our own standards of performance, and in doing so to pick and follow our own leaders. That meant, as always, Freddy.

To a Little League coach, had there been anything so absurd, Freddy would hardly have seemed the stuff of athletic stardom. Though agile enough and as good as the rest of us at throwing and catching, he was spindly of frame and of only medium size. It was his gift for sparking others that set him apart: to imagination, intelligence and unfailing good humor he added a reflexive ability to recognize what the given moment demanded, whether it was what to do on a rainy afternoon or who should do what to restore order to a chaotic ball game; even at twelve he could organize the busy energies of half a dozen boys and make something coherent and purposeful of their thrashings. One always came home from a day with him feeling the time well-spent. His genius had given us scientific research and an ambitious program to purge the United States of crime. Now it gave us the Ravens.

I have no idea how long he'd been nursing the plan, but by the time of the Forsyth County Fair, which was always in late September and for which school was closed for a day, he had instructed us to buy green felt pennants and to have the word "Ravens" sewed onto them on the spot. We duly obeyed, of course, and he then instructed us to have our mothers sew the inscribed pennants onto whatever old sweaters we planned to wear for football; and they too, by now accustomed to Freddy's programs, duly obeyed. He exerted an effortless and wholly benevolent authority; it was always obvious that he knew what everyone should do.

Thus uniformed, we were ready for practise, which, now that we were organized, occurred every afternoon, till dusk, in the Speases' backyard. The ten of us soon found our positions. Bill Williamson, Freddy's age, was fast and strong and became one halfback, Tommy Loman, much smaller but a good runner too, the other. Grady, not only tall but the best of us all at running, punting and passing, was the inevitable choice for fullback, while the various bruisers—Ozzie Young, Dan Williamson, Henry Strauss and David Thompson—made an awesome line or "forward wall," as, imitating the sports pages, we liked to call it. Tommy and I, weighing together probably less than a hundred and twenty pounds and by any measurement the smallest of the lot, were end and center respectively, sometimes the reverse, where we could do ourselves and the Ravens least harm; and it is surely unnecessary to add that Freddy took quarterback, not only to conceive strategy and call plays but to spur the slack and cheer the gloomy. Now and then he ran or passed the ball too, but others did those better and he let them; as a leader he had no rival. He was coach, trainer, manager and captain as well.

Obviously this fell something short of two-platoon capability, but the "sixty-minute man" was still the national ideal and thus ours. Drill was serious. Tackling practise against towsack dummies was soon broadened to one-on-one against each other; blocking too. Freddy was an unsparing taskmaster about fundamentals, demanding that one enhance whatever innate skills one brought to the field by perpetual work on them; so that Grady punted even oftener, Tommy drop-kicked constantly in anticipation of extra points and I centered to Freddy or Grady or Bill until I began to see the world upside down. If rain made outdoor drill impossible Freddy beckoned us to the basement to memorize plays from the blackboard easel I'd borrowed from Anne's room—plays, Freddy's ingenuity being vast, of a fiendish complexity and duplicity. We cackled to think how readily, how totally, we'd trounce our opponents.

These presently appeared, with almost Hegelian inevitability, in the form of a team of ruffians from the northern end of Buena Vista calling themselves the Carolina Cubs. Our cackling ceased. Their leader, a scruffy counterpart of Freddy, was Sanford Martin, son of the editor-in-chief of the *Winston-Salem Journal* and a gawky boy of notorious combativeness. He lived a few blocks away on Roslyn Road and had rallied to his standard nearly every boy in that corner of the neighborhood: "D" Dunn, a ferocious triple-threat back as big and as powerful as any of us; Jack Barnes and Buck Ruffin, both of whom, as I knew from experience, liked to fight, as did Marvin Ferrell, who was loud and rough and could punch like a heavyweight; Walter Gladstone, good-natured but a scrapper; Oscar Marvin, small but quick-tempered; and the immortal Willie Shore, smallest boy on either team but so fast on his feet no one could catch him to tackle once he managed to circle the end—he always played in bib overalls that remained untorn because he was never brought down. In formation, at least, with Sanford Martin calling plays and glaring at us across the line of scrimmage, the Cubs were a fearsome sight; and the fact that five of them had a piece of equipment or two heightened the threat.

They were only eight to our ten, on the other hand, and with his accustomed ingenuity Freddy found a way to preserve that advantage. Blandly indifferent to such rules as he knew, he broached the proposition that equality between sides should be determined by the combined *weights* of the players rather than by their mere *numbers*; thus by his reckoning it took ten of us, Tommy and I being unarguably small, to balance eight of them, who were unarguably hefty—though how he factored in Willie Shore, who was almost weightless, was never explained. The point was, in any case, that everyone played; and it was not until years later that I realized I owed my place in the Ravens line to Freddy's magnanimity instead of to my own modest skill.

The Cubs never won, either that year or in any of the subsequent years when, though less carefully organized, we revived our rivalry in ad hoc games. I have often wondered why. The disparity in numbers could hardly have mattered again and again. Grady and Bill Williamson notwithstanding, we boasted no brighter stars that "D" Dunn and Willie Shore, who could outrun anyone alive. Sanford Martin was a determined sparkplug and a hustling runner in his own right, and Marvin Ferrell was as combative on the football field as he was on the street. The difference, I realize now, was Freddy. Though slim and by comparison almost frail, he bore himself with such sublime assurance he must have given the impression of absolute control of the game and thus confident foreknowledge of its outcome—enough, at any rate, to strike terror in Sanford Martin's heart, which was all it took. Saturday after Saturday, spurred on by a cheering section of little sisters, we trounced them by increasingly larger margins; not even Willie Shore's speed or my fumbling and bumbling could alter the pattern of victory, which proceeded with Sophoclean inexorability. And every Saturday at noon, dust settling on the field, Sanford Martin climbed onto his rickety bicycle and led his downcast followers home to Roslyn and Arbor Roads, hair wild, shirt generally shredded, muttering above the rattle of fender and pedal, "We'll whip you next week!" But they never did. You could look it up.

12

Dream Palaces

Saturdays had a special place in our lives in more ways than one. Since Sundays were restricted to what our parents deemed ecclesiastically proper, Saturdays were the only day of the week, during the school year, when we were more or less free of some form of adult supervision, a point our fathers and mothers at least tacitly acknowledged by asking only perfunctory questions about our plans. Usually our plans were vague, in fact, if not downright shifty, for boyhood is not a time of grand designs. We almost always did the same things week after week, however, which proved gratifying to all parties: we could maintain the illusion of perfect liberty while our parents could be satisfied that we were unlikely to run risks we hadn't encountered a hundred times before.

Football or baseball was the rule on Saturday mornings—or detection, skating, kiting or tennis in their seasons—and that left all of us pleasantly sweaty, dirty and tired. In those days fathers routinely worked till noon Saturdays, so lunch had to wait till they came home—and we waited too, whether eating with friends or having them eat with us; but Saturday lunch was an occasion, decked out often with game brought to fathers by friends or fellow workers, as well as mounds of pickles and preserves and in warm weather freshly picked tomatoes, string beans, cantaloupe, watermelon, strawberries and okra. Sometimes they brought him barbecue too, but Mother wouldn't let us eat that, fearing trichinosis, no doubt, or original sin.

Lunch past, we were ready for the Saturday movie, which meant the cowboy movie. The generic term "western" must have been invented by then, but we didn't know it: the pictures we loved were about cowboys and starred cowboys, and we needed no fancier name to describe them. Getting downtown was no problem. The Buena Vista bus stopped at the corner across from Grady's—or in the middle of the block if the driver knew you, as he usually did—and it cost only seven cents and took fifteen minutes to get to Courthouse Square. Now and then a father would take us, and it was a special treat, at least in good weather, to ride in Daddy's "office car," an ancient La Salle coupe, which, though seating only two inside, was the size of a tank and had a big rumble seat reached by steel steps up one rear fender, as well as a separate locker, with its own key, for golf clubs. Sometimes as many as half a dozen of us squeezed in; we liked to yell at passersby as the La Salle made its stately progress up Brookstown Road hill, then down the long expanse of Fourth Street to the center of town. Charles Speas, who was older and presumed to know better, was invariably the loudest.

A dime got you in, for the rest of the afternoon and evening if you liked, and there were always several choices between movies. The State, Colonial and Ideal theatres lay nearly side by side along the eastern flank of Liberty Street and all showed cowboy pictures on Saturdays, though parents frowned on the Ideal because now and then it screened movies rumored to be racy; but our preference most of the time was for the State, once the official city theatre—as the inscription AVDITORIVM above the movie marquee conspicuously proclaimed—though by the 1930s replaced by sumptuous Reynolds Auditorium next to Reynolds High School. Converted to a movie house, the State still boasted a couple of balconies, including one with a separate entrance marked "colored," an orchestra pit and a huge backstage area with dressing rooms underneath; these were still in use for the weekly "stage show" on Saturday, a faded version of vaudeville, and for the occasional road-company production of some hit Broadway play or the one-night stand of one of the new dance bands playing "swing." The main draw for us was none of them, however, but the movies.

The Saturday bills, obviously designed to lure an audience of small boys and farmers in town for the day, were ambitious, or at any rate extensive. The "stage show" ordinarily opened things around one, trotting out in quick succession a juggler, a dog act, a pair of clowns and a man and woman telling each other jokes, probably off-color, that none of us got, ending usually with a musical number—a quavering baritone in a Mounties uniform calling for "Chloe" or a chubby soprano of uncertain years belting out "Avalon." This was boring stuff, on the whole, at least for small boys, and we were relieved when the stage cleared, the lights dimmed and the curtain rose again—first for a run of trailers announcing coming attractions, then for a cartoon or two, followed by a comedy short, Laurel and Hardy or Charlie Chase or Edgar Kennedy, then at last the latest episode of whatever adventure serial was in progress, Buster Crabbe as Tarzan or Flash Gordon, Ralph Byrd as Dick Tracy, the Three Mesquiteers, the original filmed Lone Ranger, the Green Hornet; a bonus delight came every three or four months when one serial ended and another began, giving us a double feature as well as an inexpressible thrill. Grady called serials "chapters" and discussed the mysterious cliff-hangers upon which each installment but the last ended with the solemnity customarily reserved for metaphysical paradoxes; and we argued endlessly about the plausibility with which the heroes' dilemmas were resolved. We liked to sit high up in the balcony near the projection booth; but so did the country folk, ripe with the sweat so familiar in a time before deodorants attained common use. Once, at a critically suspenseful moment during a "chapter," one farmer's galluses popped loose in a seat in front of Grady and flew back to slap him across the face; he yelled and jumped halfway to the ceiling, but his principal complaint afterward was that he'd missed seeing how Flash freed himself from whatever trap Ming the Merciless had sprung on him that week.

The main event was still to come; and when finally the curtain fell and rose again it must have been nearly two, if not past it. Feature films were shorter then, however, especially the low-budget cowboy films designed to fit a double bill when necessary. They were known as "B" films, in contrast to the "A" films, starring bigger names and made on bigger budgets, that were the principal fare of the fancier movie houses. "B" films were shot quickly, often in a week or so, and relied heavily on stock footage we must have seen again and again—galloping posses, gunfights along the dusty canyons of narrow mountain passes, stagecoaches in flight, bellowing Indians in pursuit; but we knew nothing of that and would scarcely have cared anyway, for what we cared about were particular cowboys wearing particular costumes reenacting the particular rituals we had learned to love and expect. Tom Mix, by our time near the end of his screen career, not only was a nimble rider but had a special trick of throwing his right leg across Tony's *neck* in comic dismounting scenes. Buck Jones wore buckskins, huge silver spurs and a grim deadpan expression we'd have thought ourselves betrayed to see softened by anything as sissy as an emotion; he sometimes used a pump gun instead of his Colt, and when the Daisy Company put a BB replica called the "Buck Jones Special" on the market we all wanted one. Colonel Tim McCoy wore a white hat and an air of lethal calm, and all of his pictures featured scenes in which he talked to Indians, a skill the movie magazines assured his fans he really possessed; while Ken Maynard, who wore a white hat too and whose black hair was slicked to a part as precise as a razor slash, may have been the trickiest horseman of them all, his specialty being to hurdle from one side to the other of a galloping horse as he dodged bullets or arrows. We had little respect for cowboys who carried two guns, thinking it a vainglorious display, though why we failed to apply the same severe sartorial standard to their fancy shirts, tight britches and ornamented boots I cannot imagine. We despised singing cowboys, though Gene Autry and Roy Rogers came along in the late '30s; and we thought of John Wayne as only another featured player, like James Ellison or Max Terhune, in serials. It seems never to have occurred to us that stunt men and doubles might be doing the really dangerous tricks or that the plots of cowboy films followed a pattern of deadly mechanical repetition. With the innate conservatism of childhood we hated change or surprise, adored certainty and predictability, and thus expected and welcomed the repetition of familiar stories. Myth was everything.

So powerful was it, in fact, that now and then it burst the modest bonds of the "B" film to move onto the more prestigious theatres in "A" films starring such leading players as Gary Cooper, Errol Flynn and Randolph Scott. The State, converted from civic auditorium to movie house, was dingy and no more than functional; but five blocks west, on fashionable Fourth Street, the Carolina Theatre showed only "A" pictures and looked the part. Built in 1928 as part of a skyscraper complex housing a hotel, apartments and stores as well, the Carolina was designed as a movie palace, and though it had an orchestra pit and some backstage space its emphasis was on the projection and viewing of films. Baroque and plush, it boasted ground-level seating for nearly a thousand as well as two balcony levels for white patrons plus the inevitable "colored" balcony reached through its own box office and elevator on Marshall Street. Ornate curtained boxes, never occupied and probably fake, adorned the side walls; the proscenium stage and curtain were perfectly scaled to the projection ratio of the time; and the magnificent statue of a nude woman only lightly veiled below the waist, probably plaster, capped the arch, drawing the upturned gaze of generations of Winston-Salem males, the youthful members of which, in the years before *Playboy* robbed the world of mystery, spent much of their time wondering what naked women really looked like. The ticket-taker and ushers wore gray mess jackets over boiled shirts with wing collars and formal black bow ties, and even children were shown to their seats behind discreetly shielded flashlights. Popcorn and candy bars were neither sold nor allowed at the Carolina, whose gilded lobby and mezzanine, decked out with ferns, reeked class, even at a dime a ticket (a quarter once one passed twelve). Patrons called it "elegant" and expected more uplifting entertainment from it than could be found in the roughhouse antics of Buck Jones or Ken Maynard.

The "A" westerns shown at the Carolina came two decades too soon for the literary pretensions of *High Noon* and *Shane*, but they were plenty high-toned. Some of the biggest male stars of the day occasionally deigned to make one, and many proved successful at playing cowboys, especially when the studios dressed their efforts with elaborate locations or sets, reasonably coherent stories and scripts and "A"-film directors like Cecil B. DeMille, John Ford, Bill Wellman and

Raoul Walsh. One of my clearest early movie memories is of Richard Barthelmess playing an American Indian in *Massacre*. I must have seen Randolph Scott in *Wagon Wheels* and George O'Brien, who'd been big in the silents, in *The Golden West* at about the same time; and within a year or so both donned leather leggings and coonskin caps, Scott to play Hawkeye in *The Last of the Mohicans*, O'Brien to portray Hawkeye's historical model, Daniel Boone, in an ambitious film biography bearing that title. Richard Dix had a huge success in *Cimarron*, another big-budget "A" western shown at the Carolina and indeed sooner or later—since Hollywood was turning out nearly three hundred pictures a year to meet the demands of an American audience whose members, scholars tell us, went to the movies at least twice, on average, a week—few stars, major or minor, could resist trying a western or two.

But the "A" western for which I retain the fondest memory starred Gary Cooper as *The Plainsman*. The title character actually was Wild Bill Hickok, hardly a cowpuncher or sod-buster, and like most of DeMille's "historical" pageants *The Plainsman* was short on truth and long on fiction. But Cooper made Hickok so glamorous and virtuous we were converted temporarily to carrying two guns, worn butt forward, like Wild Bill's; and with Jean Arthur as Calamity Jane and serial star Jimmy Ellison as Buffalo Bill, Hickok's crony, not to mention Indians charging up a shallow creekbed, Custer's Last Stand and the murder of Wild Bill by Jack McCall in a

Deadwood saloon, the picture made rational criticism irrelevant. I would happily sit through it again tomorrow, perhaps twice, to see Hickok's two-handed draw when he knocks off Charles Bickford, the villainous gunrunner, in the penultimate scene.

What is clear in retrospect is that we lived by movies—not just by them, either, but for them and in them, and not just the cowboy movies that were our cynosure but all movies. Movies were fresh, new, vivid, plentiful and blessedly cheap; television did not exist, legitimate theatre was unavailable and radio was fun but limited. Some of us read books and some listened to music, but the chief popular entertainment of the time was the motion picture; and the motion-picture industry, universally known as Hollywood, obligingly served up an endless smorgasbord, endlessly refreshed, of films of every sort for every taste. Purists will argue, and correctly, that Hollywood's astonishing diversity carefully avoided direct handling of subjects or ideas feared to provoke objection or to arouse controversy. Sexual themes were treated with special skittishness, as were political issues likely to offend the sensibilities of American business: censorship by both official state and local boards and the industry itself was commonplace and often rigid. Within its self-created timidity, however, Hollywood managed to produce its share of movies depicting a broader range of sexual matters than it publicly admitted, inventing a variety of cinematic subtleties—the discreet fade-out or cutaway, the use of inanimate images as metaphors to imply what could not be shown—that effectively communicated taboos; and in the "populist" pictures of Frank Capra and his imitators, as in the topical thrillers produced by Warner Brothers, many more of the raw political problems of the Depression era—lynching, unemployment, poverty, hopelessness, crime, the powerlessness of the Little Man and the cruelty of Big Business—reached the mass audience than was generally acknowledged.

I do not mean to profess, of course, that we boys were conscious of such matters, though we could scarcely have missed them altogether. What we loved in the movies was the rich fantasy of vicarious adventure, plus all the romantic emotion that accompanied it: the dream of heroism, the destruction of evil, the excitement of the exotic and the legendary. Westerns gave us those satisfactions, even the "B" westerns we watched on Saturdays; but during the '30s Hollywood was particularly ambitious too in producing filmed versions of famous books. Mother would not let me see Frederic March's celebrated portrayal of *Dr. Jekyll and Mr. Hyde*, alas, but with my friends I sat spellbound through *Frankenstein* and *Dracula*. They were followed by a splendid succession of literary movies, most drawn from books especially loved by boys, *David Copperfield* and *A Tale of Two Cities, Treasure Island* and *Romeo and Juliet, Mutiny on the Bounty* and *The Hound of the Baskervilles, Clive of India* and *Lost Horizon, Becky Sharp* and *Cap-*

tain Blood. My favorites, seen again and again, were Walter Abel's version of *The Three Musketeers*, Errol Flynn's *Robin Hood*, both remakes of famous Douglas Fairbanks silent successes, and the Ronald Colman edition of *The Prisoner of Zenda*, which—with Raymond Massey as Black Michael and Fairbanks *fils* swashbuckling his way through the scenery as Rupert of Hentzau, plus a cast of impeccably right actors and actresses in the other parts, as well as mystery, romance, abundant swordplay and a terrific castle for Colman to storm—stirred me to my toenails; it had everything a small boy dreamed of. When years later I chanced across it once more in Calcutta, where I was waiting to come home after nearly four years of war, it was as heart-stopping as ever.

13

Simple Pleasures

The movies apart, entertainment and amusement were scarce and mostly self-created. Like other Southern cities Winston-Salem offered little diversion beyond high school football and could boast virtually no public culture beyond the limited collection of the Carnegie Library. Apart from the four or five annual concerts of the Civic Music Association, on whose board Mother sat for years, the only music was that of the occasional student recital at the Salem College

School of Music, the inevitable December presentation of Handel's *Messiah* by Miss Nancy Ann Harris and the weekly summer concerts in Salem Square (with pink lemonade served from zinc washtubs) by the Moravian Band. Except for a yearly children's play by the Junior League, of whose Winston-Salem chapter Mother was an early member, the only available theatre came in the form of a one-nighter now and then by the touring companies offering road productions of this or that Broadway success. Art galleries were unknown and the only museum was Salem's, open one afternoon before Christmas primarily, as I remember it, to exhibit the stagecoach said to have been occupied by George Washington on his Southern tour of 1791. The WPA offered infrequent art classes at old West End School, but because the artists teaching them often failed to show up they were poorly attended.

Children were expected to entertain themselves and to be imaginative at doing so, and they were expected to do it, for the most part, at home. Evenings were brief, built around homework, if any remained, and half an hour participating in the national postprandial ritual of listening to the radio. Though still only a decade old, radio was already a nearly universal American preoccupation, but the receivers themselves—Philcos, Emersons, Stromberg-Carlsons and dozens of others now forgotten—had yet to be reduced to miniature, personal stature; having a radio of one's own was rare, and mostly the family gathered to listen to a single set, in living room or library, that was usually large and unwieldy, an appliance that manufacturers sought with great ingenuity to disguise as furniture—the "cathedral" style, nowadays a pop symbol of the '30s, being only the most familiar. We had a succession of them in the library or "back living room," as my parents called it, including a cathedral Philco that occupied a small table beside my father's armchair and a floor "console" that looked a lot like an old-fashioned icebox; but the extraordinary intimacy with which Americans of every class took radio to their hearts made one quickly forget that the odd maple or oak thing with the tiny dial was really only a front for a bewildering complex of tubes, condensers and wires that mysteriously, if tuned with the utmost delicacy, filled the room with the voices of Lowell Thomas and "Amos 'n Andy."

Some of my friends' parents developed an attachment to the nightly newscasts of Boake Carter and H. V. Kaltenborn, but for my parents, and thus for us, no one could rival Lowell Thomas. One of my adventure books, *Men of Daring*, depicted him as an authentic hero, in fact, who'd made movies in the trenches of the Western Front and discovered Lawrence of Arabia, and with his chocolaty baritone and vigorous, confident delivery he certainly seemed it. He came on at seven—"live," of course, since the taped delay did not exist—and when he signed off fifteen minutes later with his famous trademark, "And so long until tomorrow," Americans *knew* they'd been told everything important that had happened in the world that day. He had an authority not even Walter Cronkite, projected by a far more sophisticated technology, could surpass.

"Amos 'n Andy" was something else—a sound drama, comic but boasting a continuous narrative, that I realize now perfectly demonstrated radio's remarkable ability to stimulate listeners' imaginations by the simplest of means: two voices and a few effects mechanically produced. It is derided nowadays as unforgivably racist, and so, by its depiction of the American Negro as typically ignorant, shiftless, lazy and cunning, it may have been; but it is hard for me to believe that Gosden and Correll, the white vaudevillians who created it, intended cruelty by their broad humor, and in any case its racial stereotypes were characteristic of the stage and movies of their time. It also seems worth remembering that Amos, at least, was portrayed as both intelligent and good, and that it was his competence, not a white man's, that again and again pulled Andy's overheated irons out of the fire. Gosden and Correll were gifted actors, whatever one's view of their product, able to shape not only the two main characters but a whole supporting cast—most notably the Kingfish and Lightnin'—into such credible people one halfway expected to meet them next day on the street; and their Harlem taxi office had a solidity, in the mind's eye, few movie sets could rival. They did it alone, moreover, with their own voices enacting every character who entered the tale.

We had other radio favorites, though none their equal. The rural "Lum 'n Abner," a sort of white hayseed counterpart of "Amos 'n Andy," was one. Jack Benny's Sunday night show was another, as were the similar variety half-hours of Fred Allen, Phil Baker and Ed Wynn, and "Fibber McGee and Molly," as well as the Edgar Bergen and Charlie McCarthy program, caught our fancies too as radio continued to stretch itself throughout the '30s; and there were numerous afternoon shows for children—"Little Orphan Annie," "Red Davis," "Tom Mix"—we sometimes caught on rainy days. But weeknights were strict in Buena Vista: until we were nearing our teens we were sent to bed, if not to sleep, once "Amos 'n Andy" was over. Radio was fun, but there were other things in the world.

Uppermost among them was reading. Scotch and purposeful in everything, Mother expected Anne and me to read nightly before turning out our lights—and we did, initiating the habit, at least in my case, of a lifetime. She and Daddy read all the time, morning and evening newspapers, a dozen magazines, an endless stream of books, the Bible and commentaries on it, and they took it for granted that we would be readers too. When the built-in bookcases covering the rear wall of the back living room were filled, the new books all of us brought home spilled over into the living room and then upstairs into a second expanse along the wall of the hallway, and our rooms bulged with books. It was a family trait, I suppose, transferred from my grandparents' house in Fincastle; and though Mother complained more than once that the foundations were certain to buckle sooner or later from the accumulation, she did not stop bringing new books in, nor did the rest of us. We borrowed them from libraries and friends, stole them from Granddaddy, ordered them through the mail and bought them from booksellers; we gave and got them as presents and often spent Christmas evening excitedly turning the pages of the latest haul. Books were the coin of the realm, the source of wisdom, and we never had enough.

Mother's education in classical and English literature gave her a pronounced inclination that way, not to mention a bottomless well of improving quotations for every contingency; but she read the popular fiction of the time too, enthusiastic about *Anthony Adverse, So Red the Rose, Gone with the Wind* and *Rebecca*, and she read Hemingway, Fitzgerald, Wilder and Wolfe, the writers of her own generation, dutifully though with less real interest and much bafflement, for her taste was firmly grounded in the nineteenth century and the big, solid social novels of Dickens, Thackeray, George Eliot and Henry James. She tried to interest herself in Proust and Virginia Woolf but with little success. Daddy, however, had no feeling for fiction; he liked to read history, especially American history and biography, Marquis James on Andrew Jackson and

Sam Houston, the early naval histories of Samuel Eliot Morrison, Douglas Freeman's multi-volume life of Lee and then, through the careers of Lee's subordinates, Freeman's history of the Army of Northern Virginia, its battles and blunders. Eventually he became an amateur Civil War expert, in fact, hard on Longstreet and eager to demonstrate that hapless commander's shortcomings and mistakes, which I suspect were clearer to him because of Longstreet's postwar defection to Republicanism; but at least it was never difficult to find him a birthday present.

My own taste was predictable: I loved adventure, the more swashbuckling the better, and quickly developed a second sense for books that offered it. They surrounded me anyway, the swordplay fare of which boys' books had been built since the explosion of mass fiction in the early nineteenth century, brought down to Winston-Salem to overflow my shelves from the overflowing shelves in Fincastle where Mother's three brothers had dog-eared and devoured them during their own boyhood days. I formed an early fondness for John Esten Cooke's lurid tale of the Civil War *Surry of Eagle's Nest*, certain that romantic Turner Ashby looked exactly like Daddy and Jeb Stuart like my Uncle Stuart, then only a few years out of V.M.I. and dashing on horseback. There were Henty and Alger and series books like the Tarzan novels, a new one each year as my uncles grew up, and the Dick Prescott line, *Dick Prescott's First Year at West Point* and its sequels depicting his second year, and his third and fourth, and then at last his time as a second lieutenant (*Trading the Gray for Shoulder Straps*), as a first lieutenant, as a captain. The Tom Swift books were exciting and also, to my delight, apparently innumerable, and there were a number of pirate and sailor books through which I first learned of the exploits of Henry Morgan and Captain Kidd, John Paul Jones and Stephen Decatur; and a pair of breathtaking stories about Boy Scouts, saving families lost in the wilderness, whose titles I have forgotten. Ralph Connors's novels of growing up in Canada, *Glengarry School Days* and *The Man from Glengarry*, took my fancy, portraying a rural life I could only imagine, and Henry Shute's autobiographical books about his New England boyhood, *Plupy, The Real Diary of a Real Boy* and *Sequil*, became favorites for life. But nothing made a deeper impression on my already vivid prepubescent imagination than *The Three Musketeers* and *Treasure Island*, copies of which my grandparents gave me as birthday presents at nine or ten. I still see D'Artagnan as Milo Winter painted him in the Windermere series, Long John Silver as N. C. Wyeth and Frank Godwin painted him for the two editions I ultimately owned. I still recall with a thrill the hot summer afternoon in Fincastle when I complained of boredom and Granddaddy reached behind him to hand down *The Valley of Fear* and thus introduced me to the permanent good company of Sherlock Holmes. That same summer he also called my attention to *The Prisoner of Zenda* and its sequel *Rupert of Hentzau*, both of which I read again and again; and when the Ronald Colman movie of *Prisoner* promptly appeared I knew I had cause to envy no man.

Much of this was trash, of course, but boys prefer the color and action trash provides to the more meditative pleasures. Even trashier were comic books, which first appeared in the late '30s, and Big Little Books, which were sold at Woolworth's and Kress', the 5-and-10s that were my favorite haunts in downtown Winston-Salem. Now treasured as cult items, Big Little Books were, in effect, hardcover reprints of popular comic-strip episodes, key frames with their balloons removed alternating page by page with a written narrative tracing the story: Little Orphan Annie, Dick Tracy, Buck Rogers, a rousing account of the Lewis and Clark expedition lifted from a newspaper strip called "Highlights of History." Their stiff board format was square, about four by four, and they were invariably at least a couple of inches thick. A rival series of Little Big Books in slightly more rectangular format was drawn from movies of the time—*Les Miserables* with Frederic March, *The Lost Patrol* with Victor McLaglen—and featured stills from the films alternating with drastically condensed versions of the tales. There were also Big Big Books, dime-store volumes in standard book format, but they never quite caught on like the smaller ones, which neatly lined my bookshelves and which I lent and traded, like all of my friends, as jealously as if they were illuminated mediaeval manuscripts. Big Little and Little Big Books sold for a quarter, which made them big-ticket items during the Depression, and nowadays fetch extravagant prices as collector's items. I saved none of mine, alas, though I still have my boyhood copies of *The Three Musketeers, Treasure Island,* the Tarzan and Plupy books and *The Prisoner of Zenda*, not to mention—perhaps most precious of all because it reminds me so vividly of my grandfather—*The Valley of Fear*, with its blood-curdling revelation: "Birdy Edwards is here. I am Birdy Edwards."

When my bedside light went out, seldom later than eight-thirty, the house and street seemed to subside into slumber too. My parents rarely stayed up past eleven, though they liked to play a few hands of cards and listen to the radio themselves before settling into their invariable hour or two of reading. The house cooled slowly—rapidly if I forgot to feed the stoker—and from my bed I could hear it creak and groan as its wooden skeleton shrank and the clank of the radiator beneath my window as the heat left it for the night. A universal truth of the day, no doubt handed down by my parents' Victorian forebears and by them no doubt taken from the English, was that it was unhealthy to sleep in warm air, the result being the sleeping porches at my grandparents' house and the open windows at ours. Anne and I were deeply bundled beneath layer upon layer of blankets, quilts and comforters, and in wintertime we wore flannel pyjamas, so that neither we nor our friends, all of whom slept in the same Spartan fashion, were cold ourselves at all; but an inch beyond our noses the air was arctic, and getting up to go to the bathroom was torture. We would catch, we were told, fewer colds that way. The custom had its infrequent pleasures, to be sure. It was lovely to rise in that polar cold on Christmas morning to go trembling downstairs to an open fire and all the glittering surprises before it; and when, in the early morning hours of Easter, one was wakened by the sound of a brass chorale and pulled the shade aside to see the Moravian Band rousing the city's sleepers beneath the cone of yellow light at the corner, the freezing air deepened the beauty of the occasion.

My parents at a family camp,
Craig's Creek, Virginia, circa. 1920.
My father is still wearing parts of his World War I uniform.

My sister Anne and I in front of the house at 608 Arbor Road, 1930.
My sailor suit is the only garment I ever owned in
which I took absolute satisfaction.

The house at 707 Oaklawn Avenue,
photographed during a rare North Carolina snow,
circa. 1935

Freddy Speas,
who organized everything,
1934

Tommy Speas
with my new bike,
1934

CAMP HANES, 1936.
left to right: Grady Southern, Carlyle Cooke, John Cunningham, the author

THE RAVENS, 1934.
left to right: Tommy Speas, Grady Southern, David Thompson, Osborne Young, Tommy Lowman, Freddy Speas, Bill Williamson, the author (visible with magnification), Henry Strauss, Dan Williamson

THE CAROLINA CUBS, the Ravens' weekly opponents. 1934.
left to right: "D" Dunn, Willie Shore (world's fastest runner), Walter Gladstone, Jack Barnes, Marvin Ferrell, Sanford Martin (Cubs captain, manager), Oscar Marvin, Buck Ruffin

14

Grace Abounding

If Saturdays were freedom, Sundays were prison. Since God had yet to discover the South, or at any rate the privileged classes of the South, religion was relatively mild and thus relatively pleasant; but it played a central role in most families' lives and was in many respects more important to them than it would seem in later decades when it became more conspicuous. Sundays were too.

My parents were Presbyterians, and Presbyterians of Scotch lineage, which meant a rigorously rational theology and tradition, and both had been reared in the Presbyterian church; but they came from families split between Presbyterianism and Episcopalianism. My father's Paxton forebears were bedrock Scotch Presbyterians, but on his father's side lay many Episcopalians, and his sisters were Episcopalians too. Ecclesiastically, at least, my mother's ancestors showed no more consistency: the McDowells, who were visibly and characteristically Scotch, were Episcopalians, while the Beckleys, who were just as typically English, were Presbyterians—though my grandfather McDowell, alone in his large clan, insisted on being a Presbyterian. None of this made much sense historically or culturally and may have been simply a matter of temperamental affinity, like preferring Carl Hubbell to Dizzy Dean or Gary Cooper to Cary Grant, but to a small boy it was a bewildering muddle made more confusing in the summertime when, in Fincastle, we attended the Presbyterian service one Sunday, the Episcopal the next, and found the same congregation at each. The explanation was that since neither church had a minister every week, they had sensibly arranged their schedules to dovetail; but it left certain major issues of faith and practice unanswered.

Presbyterians were scarce in North Carolina, though, and Episcopalians scarcer still. The latter could fill but a single church in Winston-Salem, beautiful St. Paul's overlooking the western reaches of the city from the eminence of Summit Street; but it was a wealthy parish boasting an abundance of the professionally and socially prominent among its communicants. Presbyterians did somewhat better, with First Presbyterian Church a substantial congregation downtown and two small satellite or mission churches in East and North Winston; but its powerful role in civic and political affairs, disproportionate to its numbers, derived from the fact that besides old Winston families it drew a significant part of its membership from the ruling executive and professional class, including R. J. and Will Reynolds. Somewhat like a mediaeval suzerain, "Mr. Dick" eventually withdrew to create his own tiny, exquisite church at Reynolda, and though always a little the child of First Presbyterian, it was a breakaway church with a perennial appeal for those who liked their Presbyterianism small and exclusive. Both churches were rich, in any case, as was St. Paul's, and all three were citadels of dignity, formality and—though this was never said, of course— gentility.

A sociologist could have deduced the strata of Winston-Salem society by studying the congregations of the various churches as they mingled to chat on church steps and walks after Sunday morning services; but he would have found some things bafflingly inconsistent with denominational stereotypes. Baptists dominated North Carolina and Winston-Salem, and the nominally genteel considered their religion too emotional for any but the commoner lot; but a number of the city's eminent lawyers, doctors and businessmen were pillars of big, florid First Baptist Church on Fifth Street, and none suggested the slightest embarrassment at being Baptists, for many were graduates of Wake Forest College or its law or medical schools and were proud of "Old Wake's" intellectual tradition. Methodists, almost as numerous, were clearly numerous enough to make Centenary Methodist Church the biggest church in town. In its handsome stone sprawl a block west of First Baptist, it had the Grays and many of the Haneses and thus was rarely in want. Smaller Baptist and Methodist churches dotted the city as well, and though none rivaled Centenary's congregational power, they helped swell their denomination's rolls. Moravians had their place too but it was a special place, an enclave that never proselytized, and Lutherans, Christian Scientists, Roman Catholics, Greek Orthodox, Jews and what shards existed of other faiths had to make do with tiny congregations of minimal influence and no more social standing than Hottentots.

This was snobbish but standard. Unconcerned with the-ological niceties, or even theology, Americans chose their churches then as now out of the accident of birth or from a desire to confirm or acquire the trappings of a particular social milieu. Probably the former was more often the case, for until World War II mobility was limited and one tended to stay where one started, in every sense, so that one tended to be, say, Baptist because one was born or married a Baptist; but gossip also hinted from time to time that this rising couple or that had forsworn their native Methodism for the fancier ways of the Episcopalians. Skeptics and "freethinkers" no doubt existed, like hookworm and malaria, but in the South, where social curiosity was endemic and a profession of Protestantism in some form or other a badge of orthodoxy, churchgoing was nearly universal.

Religion, in fact, *was* churchgoing, being substantially a matter of social intercourse and the visible evidence of social position; the fine points of faith that distinguished the sects were rarely mentioned and probably unknown to any but the most learned of their adherents. Everyone knew that Baptists baptized by immersion and many had been told that Presbyterianism's bicameral lay government was the model for the American system, but the denominations' differences on whether sin was redeemed by faith or works or a blend of both interested few and none enough to provoke discussion. Church was a habit, was a social custom, was what one did on Sundays, like putting on one's finest clothes, picking up the Sunday *New York Times* at the Robert E. Lee Hotel cigarstand and sitting down to the largest meal of the week, usually with a spinster schoolteacher or two for company.

The secularization of religious life was complete, in short; the rest was behavior. Here convention ruled, and the conventions a family followed were determined by denominational custom, which came down, in the end, to the customs of class. Some were severe. Carl and Gene Holbrook, who lived down the street, were the sons of a teller at the Wachovia Bank and would have seemed, on the face of it, improbable exemplars of backwoods Puritanism; but their father was the son of a saloon keeper—in the days before Prohibition settled upon Winston-Salem—and he was a hard-shell Baptist to boot, so they could do nothing on Sundays, not even ride their bikes in the afternoon, and were confined to their front steps, watching the rest of us, heathen and hedonistic, from pale, pinched faces above their tieless church shirts buttoned to the neck, whispering, when urged to revolt, that their father was also liberal with the belt.

This was no problem for Grady or Tommy or Sonny or me, for once Sunday school, church and the interminable Sunday dinner were past we were allowed almost as much freedom as we enjoyed weekdays. This was less than total, to be sure. Parents liked to call on friends, especially elderly friends, on Sunday afternoons, and children were expected to accompany them and only rarely were excused from that hated duty; all of us spent more time than we liked in dark, overheated Victorian parlors, reeking of lavender and mildew, listening to ancient widows extolling the brilliance of that morning's sermon and its frock-coated delivery by Dr. This or Dr. That—for the big Winston churches commanded the most erudite of the South's Protestant clergy. Soggy lemon cookies, generally alongside tepid tea, were also a constant. This was less than the freedom of the street, for which we yearned. "Blue laws," which lasted until World War II, kept movies closed and forestalled any sports event larger than a game of catch in the backyard. These were holdovers from a stricter past, but my parents and my friends' parents, though seldom strict themselves, accepted them without question as a norm of civilized life and would have regarded the open theatres and ball games of big-city Sundays as Babylonian license only too typical of "Yankees."

Our affiliation was with the First Presbyterian Church, which stood with Victorian dignity, rectitude and ugliness on Cherry Street in the heart of downtown Winston. The main building, a dark brick oval with darker pews and imposing stained-glass windows front and side, was a turn-of-the-century replacement for an earlier, more modest building and was replaced itself in the 1970s; it expressed perfectly the solidity, high seriousness and unimpeachable business, professional and social superiority of its members. Will Maslin, a tall, elderly town bachelor, presided over all ushers from inside his black frock coat at the center front door, and Mrs. Horace Sebring, a vast, pneumatic redhead of legendary bossiness, played the organ and ruled the choir from a cramped loft directly behind the pulpit, casting her cold eye upon the congregation, as it cast an equally cold eye on her, from a mirror above the console. Despite her iron fist, however, and apart from an occasional star soloist like Brooks Bynum, a young Winston basso whose resemblance to Errol

Flynn stirred many a feminine heart, it remained a choir of singular ineptitude, heavy, poorly balanced and frequently off-key; though when I voiced that sentiment on the way home Mother, who frequently expressed it even more acerbically, blandly reminded me that it was "easier to criticize than to do." This logic failed to deal with the issue, of course, but it shut me up.

The fact was that the First Presbyterian Church was, after their family, the center of my parents' lives. From their first days in North Carolina they had played busy parts in it and by the time I was a boy and aware, both were important figures in its activities. Mother was a regular circle and auxiliary member, often an officer and several times auxiliary president, and she played a similar part in the Presbyterial. Daddy, while still young, taught Sunday school, became its superintendent and was raised to the diaconate, then became a member of the session, and a permanent elder, in his fiftieth year, 1936; he soon was named clerk of session and served in that role for the rest of his life, invariably acting as clerk of the congregation when it met as well. It is probably unnecessary to add that their attendance at church was as regular as the legendary routine by which his neighbors set their clocks to Kant's daily passage. They often went to prayer meetings on Wednesday night and to whatever smaller worship services or business meetings were scheduled. Shortly after I joined the Boy Scouts my father dutifully took his turn on the troop committee. Visiting ministers—Dr. Ben Lacy and Dr. Taliaferro Thompson of Union Theological Seminary, in particular—seemed unarguably to take Sunday dinner with us.

I do not mean to impugn the sincerity of their faith when I note that they also had excellent practical reasons for so rich an involvement. In a time before good roads and the widespread use of automobiles made broad social connections easy, affiliation with a church was a natural way of bringing people together—especially people of like background, education and interests. Men's downtown and civic clubs and women's book, garden and bridge clubs accomplished a similar end, and for the prosperous who could afford them country clubs, still a new notion, offered a parallel social institution. But nothing equaled the churches for introducing people in a setting that combined respectability and purpose; the particular Protestant denominations, moreover, had long since assumed clearly defined class lines that were so universally understood they never needed to be made explicit. For my parents Presbyterianism was not only their birthright but their natural milieu: in the Presbyterian church—especially in the First Presbyterian Church of Winston-Salem—they mingled with the sort of people and families with whom they could feel perfectly comfortable because they had always known such people, had grown up and been to school with people like them, and shared with them, besides a faith in predestination, the confidence that all of them were well-born, well-bred, well-educated, well-dressed, well-employed and well-connected and that all of them were soberly well-intentioned. It did not invariably work out that way, Presbyterians being notoriously given to the contentious splitting of the narrowest hairs, but at least their quarrels took place within a commonly grasped context.

Our prosperous flock was led, in my earliest days, by Dr. John S. Foster, a truly terrifying figure who looked like the aged Wordsworth and was almost as sanctimonious. Obviously he ended by outraging many others with his high-handedness, for in the mid-1930s Daddy and his friend Arch Taylor, who were then the "Young Turks" of the diaconate, captained a successful movement to get rid of him; where-upon he was succeeded, after a suitable search, by Dr. John R. Cunningham, president of the Louisville Seminary, who—before moving on some years later to the presidency of Davidson College—proved to be the most successful minister in the history of the church. He was tall, handsome, formal, learned and eloquent, a reminder both physically and intellec-tually of Woodrow Wilson and his brand of enlightened Scotch Presbyterianism. He also belonged to my parents' gen-eration and shared their liberal social and political views, which helped; and though he cautioned his children against reading secular literature on Sundays, his older son John, my exact contemporary, blithely ignored him and became a close friend. It was a matter of dark record that during the morning service one Sunday not long after Dr. Cunningham's arrival, John and I, exploring mysterious closets and cubbyholes behind the choir loft, fell into the organ while Dr. Cunningham preached and my father nodded gravely from his pew. "For of such," intoned the good doctor from the pulpit, "is the kingdom of Heaven," and everything in the pipes gave a *whump*.

We were only punished, as I remember, with a stern look; but in fact Presbyterianism was punishment enough. It was somehow worse than a beating to be perpetually so dutiful, so high-minded, so serious about a world so obviously absurd, and the constant stress on hearing and heeding the admonitions of conscience was enough to set a small boy quite deliberately on the road to Death Row. Yet though my parents took all this quite for granted, they were anything but stern themselves. They were witty and merry most of the time, even Sundays, and never ostentatiously carried Bibles to church or quoted Scripture to point a moral. At home our only religious practises were to bless meals and to say the bedtime prayers all children were taught.

Churchgoing was crucial, however, the more the better. Besides Sunday school and church Sunday mornings, which were routine and mandatory, Mother and Daddy often attended Sunday evening vespers, a shorter service, and prayer meeting Wednesday nights, which I loathed and from which, after groaning at hearing my father pray aloud, I was finally excused. But it was only a reprieve. Upon reaching adolescence I began attending the "young people's" meeting Sunday nights, supper and talk in a putatively "lighter" vein; and in this I did only what all of my friends, Baptist, Methodist, Episcopal and Moravian, did at the same time in their own churches. I sang in the children's choir, the junior choir, as a high-school senior the adult choir, all under the baleful eye of the redoubtable Mrs. Sebring.

But none of the numerous tortures devised by Presbyterianism to instill a horror of Sundays in small boys exceeded, in ingenuity or barbarity, the Shorter Catechism. There was nothing short about it except by comparison with the Longer Catechism, which I knew only by rumor and was spared; and when set alongside the Child's Catechism it looked as daunting as it was. All three had been created in an earlier era to teach Presbyterian dogma by rote, and by my childhood were all but forgotten by any but the most fervent Scotch communicants. As it happened, however, Mother was one of the few whose long memories kept ancient custom alive. As a bright child at the turn of the century she had "said" the Shorter Catechism herself, as her father had, and was determined, now that I was ten and thus in full possession of reason, to bring me too into the fear and nurture of the Lord.

The Child's and Shorter Catechisms came in pocket-sized pamphlets, the one with a pink paper cover, the other in mustard, nearly mirroring the mustard plasters of winter;

both solemnly bore the seals of Westminster and both were cast in a succession of questions and answers through which the principal beliefs and themes of the Presbyterian church were set forth. The catechist asked the questions; the child gave the answers. The hitch, alas, was that though the catechist could read, the child could not—answers had to be memorized and spoken by rote, and in the crucial test not even a syllable could be fumbled. Perfection and Presbyterianism were synonymous.

I had sailed through the Child's Catechism at six, blithely still able to memorize anything and wholly innocent of the nightmare ahead, and had just as innocently forgotten it. In this I reckoned without recognizing that in the eyes of every Presbyterian mother every Presbyterian son is a larval Presbyterian minister. Glimpses of the gleaming spires of Davidson and Hampden-Sydney, perhaps Princeton or even Edinburgh, offered tantalizing promise of ecclesiastic bliss and maternal fulfillment. The Shorter Catechism was the first step.

The actuality must have been as ghastly for her as it was for me. Each Sunday afternoon throughout the steamy summer of 1935 she sat me down on the side porch to master new blocks of questions and answers—five a week, as I remember, though it may have been, and certainly seemed, more. I was drilled till my teeth ached, and when I'd finally got the new batch down pat we'd return to the first page and re-recite all I'd learned before, so that each Sunday's drill session inevitably grew larger week by week. I became desperately angry and sullen and, though I loved her dearly, kept imagining Mother as the target of bayonet practise. Once, scheming to circumvent the hideous occasion, I contrived to lose my catechism. "No problem," she said calmly, and whipped out a fresh copy. When decades later I wrote a newspaper account of my sufferings, a reader retaliated with his own: he was the son of a Presbyterian minister, and when he fled up a tree to escape *his* catechising mother, she followed him out onto a branch without dropping an admonition.

I would like to claim that the Shorter Catechism improved my sinful character or at least familiarized me with the essentials of Presbyterian theology, but in fact I found it absolute gibberish, and still do. I "said" it perfectly one September afternoon to a kind lady named Mrs. Tully Blair, of whom I knew little beyond the fact that her husband was the best golfer in Winston-Salem, and within five minutes of leaving her house I had forgotten it almost totally. I took home a book she'd given me—"More Minute Biographies," which I loved and still have—and the next month, with high Scotch unction, the church presented me with a leatherbound Bible, which I have too but love less. As for Presbyterian dogma, I remember only the first question, "What is the chief end of man?" and its answer, "Man's chief end is to glorify God and to serve him forever"; and that made no more sense to me, then or afterward, than the notion that the moon is made of green cheese. The one real thing I gained from the Shorter Catechism was a new and enduring respect for Mother's determination.

15

Life as a Fascist

An age dominated by the instant gratifications of television has less patience than ours did for the primitive pleasures of an out-of-doors life unalleviated by labor-saving technology; so it is scarcely surprising that the Boy Scouts, with their simple idealism and stress on the robust virtues, should enjoy less popularity nowadays than they once did. Today the sight of Boy Scouts causes heads to turn, but in the 1930s no public occasion was complete without them—helping with traffic and parking, assisting pedestrians, laying on flags, escorting speakers. "Scouting," always with a capital letter, was cheap to undertake, accessible at every level, time-consuming; it more or less kept boys out of mischief by setting them increasingly difficult goals, it taught the moral values the middle classes agreed were essential to a stable society and it got its adherents out of the house on Friday nights. It was thus, for my generation of boys, a nearly universal experience.

Probably it was inevitable that Scouting was tied closely to the churches of the community. The churches' established organizations made it easy to add on boys' groups of pronounced hierarchical structure, and their adult male members constituted a natural pool of leaders, besides which the many religious affirmations of the Boy Scouts, though never explicitly denominational or even Christian, made the alliance natural. Almost every church had its troop, and to no one's surprise the bigger, richer churches produced the more visible troops. Within that general framework, however, they varied greatly in the accomplishment of major Scouting feats, and a dramatically successful troop usually owed its vitality to a vigorous scoutmaster. By everyone's reckoning the best troop in Winston-Salem was Troop 9 of Home Moravian Church. Home Moravian was a big, rich church boasting an abundance of prominent members, thus could draw on a large and perpetually replenished reservoir of lively boys; but that could have been said of at least five other churches in town. What gave Troop 9 its enviable record of Eagle Scouts and team victories at camp and in special city-wide Scouting events during Boy Scout Week was the inspired leadership of Horace Vance, a young Moravian who'd grown up in the community, been an outstanding Boy Scout himself and taken on the troop after college. Though as scoutmaster he was unpaid he seemed to work at Scouting all the time, and his troop adored him; his charisma was so great, in fact, that many boys from other churches forsook their natural allegiances to join Troop 9. It had a mystique.

So, to a lesser extent, did Troop 18 at First Baptist Church and the equally big troops, whose numbers I no longer remember, at Centenary Methodist and Calvary Moravian. All the Speases were members of Troop 18 and all, with their dependability and strong sense of duty, did well, Dixon and Charles especially, both becoming Eagle Scouts, Dixon twice, and displaying early promise. No one would have said that of me or of Troop 17 at First Presbyterian. We were a mixed bag at best, boasting a winner now and then but notorious as a group for our lackadaisical attitude toward the major accomplishments of Scouting, boys given to fun and milk-shakes more than to the attainment of the Merit Badges by which high rank was won. We had wonderful times, to be sure, and Troop 17 was never wanting for new members; but with a handful of exceptions we were a disappointment to our parents and the men of the church who made up the Troop Committee, and we were the despair of "Skipper" Vaughan-Lloyd, the city's full-time Scout Executive, whose face invariably fell when one of us looked in on him at his trim little office at City Hall.

We had no complaints to excuse our casual Scouting. When in the early '30s—thanks to Kate Bitting Reynolds, wife of "Mr. Will"—a new educational building went up to replace the old one behind the church proper, neither money nor thought was spared to support the Boy Scouts, perhaps in the hope that an ideal den would produce ideal boys. A small wing, with its own outside door, was built on the north side of the handsome stone structure, holding inside it a beautifully paneled troop room, complete with flags and framed monograms and a bronze Boy Scout emblem on the walls as well as a big closet for storing the paraphernalia required for knot-tying, camp cooking and semaphore drill, all of which symbolized Scouting's immersion in the arcane skills of the wilderness. Many of Winston-Salem's leading Boy Scouts mastered them, not to mention fire-building and camping and life-saving; but they were not from Troop 17. At Troop 17 the expensive equipment of the trade went admired and wholly unused, handsome gear of the finest manufacture gathering dust in the troop's elegant closet.

Things began for me on an appropriately convivial note. Within a week or so of turning twelve in May 1937 I learned my knots from the legendary Henry Magie, an elfin, elderly Scot who'd once been a sailor and now served on the Troop Committee, memorized the Scout's Oath and Scout Laws, was taken to buy a uniform at the Frank Stith store and found myself sworn Tenderfoot—i.e., a legitimate and official member of Troop 17, of which I'd been an illicit and unofficial member for months. All serious Scouting was immediately set aside, however, with Scoutmaster Jim Little's announcement that he was taking us all for a weekend at his alma mater, the University of North Carolina at Chapel Hill. He was precisely the sort of leader boys like us dreamed of: we had discipline and duty enough and to spare at home and school, and it was the last thing Jim Little had on his mind as well. He must then have been in his late twenties or early thirties, a big florid fellow who always reminded me of Robin Hood's Little John, at a time in his life, presumably, of ambition and enterprise; but unlike more zealous scoutmasters he seemed to prefer good times to Merit Badges, and that suited the Troop 17 tradition handsomely. He liked throwing weenie-roasts and buying everyone Cokes at the drugstore after Friday-night meetings; but I never remember taking an advancement test from him. Hauling a dozen rowdy, pubescent boys off to Carolina for the weekend—rather than leading them on a nature hike—was his style of Scouting.

The frolic gathered momentum in Chapel Hill. Either through misinformation or misunderstanding the maintenance people had prepared the visiting teams' room at the gymnasium for seventy or eighty—that many neatly made-up cots lined the walls, and we spent the first hour, and many more when we ran out of other things to do, using them as trampolines to move, one by one, from north end to south and back again. Jim Little's plans for us were hardly intellectual, in any case; he'd arranged for us to take in a first-class tennis tournament, starring the Rood boys and Arch Henderson, and to swim in the new Olympic pool across campus, and Saturday night we went to a Carolina Playmakers' outdoor performance, a first for us all, of *The Merry Wives of Windsor*, which we found pleasantly bawdy. Mostly, though, he let us roam as we liked. We discovered the Arboretum (and watched couples necking there), and Berk Ingram ran down a town drugstore where the milkshakes were immense. We took our meals for nickels and dimes at the ancient university cafeteria, Swain Hall, which we instantly learned to call "Swine Hall." The excitement of bouncing the night away kept anyone from sleeping, no one took off his uniform except to swim, and we came home Sunday evening looking like the casualties of a defeated army: George Montague had torn his uniform, Tag had bent his glasses and only Bill Ashby, who went on to become an Eagle Scout and a graduate of West Point, remained presentable. But everyone agreed— parents possibly excepted—that the trip had been a great success.

It was also, as events proved, a representative, indeed prophetic beginning to my years as a Boy Scout. After a year or so Jim Little left us—no doubt to make his way in the real world—and was succeeded by Horace Sebring. Mr. Sebring was the sort of man no one was ever known to call by his first name; but he was kind and patient and he struggled valiantly to raise us to the high standard set by Troops 18 and 9. Alas, he was, as Mencken said of Coolidge, a good man in a bad trade. We were a scruffy lot who trivialized, if we did not altogether corrupt, almost all who joined our ranks; and a man already burdened with a childless marriage to Mrs. Sebring, the henna-haired termagant of the choir loft, was doomed in advance by our lack of ambition and destructive energy. Honesty compels the additional admission that for him or anyone else to pretend to "replace" Jim Little was sacrilege.

He persevered, however, and though Troop 17 never became a notable example of Scouting endeavor, it gained a widespread reputation as the Winston-Salem troop freest of ambition and most devoted to pleasure. Since noble aims and hard work are more often proclaimed than actually sought after, especially by boys, we never lacked for enthusiastic members; and if almost none of us learned semaphore, firebuilding, life-saving or the secrets of the trail, Mr. Sebring could at least take genuine pride in having helped spur Bill

Ashby, Bill Anderson and Bill Plonk to do the drudgery and bide the time it took to become Eagle Scouts.

Scouting was my first experience of fascism, and like most boys I took to it heartily. It may not be wholly true, of course, that the Boy Scouts are a "paramilitary" organization, as its latter-day critics allege; but Scout uniforms, ranks, procedures and innumerable mottoes and maxims are certainly the next best things and its robust emphasis on physical strength and attainment echoes that of the Hitler Youth. Friday-night meetings—except for the eight or nine weeks of the high-school football season—were brought to order when the Senior Patrol Leader called the troop to a soldierly attention, barked out the command to recite the Scouts' Oath and followed it with an order to "give" the Scouts' Laws. After duly reminding ourselves that we were trustworthy, obedient, loyal, courteous, kind, cheerful, thrifty, brave, clean and reverent, in about that order, we sat down to his command and remained seated till told to do otherwise. I no longer remember what business consumed our ponderous deliberations, but before the passage of too much time could draw us into boredom we were set to work passing tests and slaving on merit badges—the saving reality being that, since this was Troop 17, most of us were soon fooling around looking for mischief, much to the dismay and eventual despair of Mr. Sebring, any members of the Troop Committee who happened to be present and the handful of ambitious members, like the various Bills, who had their eyes on attaining Eaglehood. The evening usually ended with a "belt line" running the length of the lower hall of the Sunday school building: hapless newcomers and miscreants charged with criminal inattention during the meeting were made to run the gauntlet of our flailing belts. This introduction to organized sadism was both immensely satisfying and, as I discovered on entering V.M.I. in 1942, relevant to life in the real world. Afterward we all raced off for Cokes at Bobbitt's Pharmacy in the Nissen Building skyscraper next door, then caught the bus home, hoping while still in the high spirits induced by the belt line to terrorize whatever bus driver we found. But we never succeeded. All of them knew all of us by name, street, block and house and yawned at our antics.

Though the conventional wisdom says otherwise, boys love authority, both to defy and obey and often both at once. Scouting provides it in an almost perfect balance of proportions: uniformed adult men or late-adolescent boys who set clear principles and rules derived from them but lack the power to make them more than advisory. Boy Scouts thus function within a well-defined code to which they may rally or against which they may chafe: a safe code, in short, that establishes both limits and the room to breach them without risk. As a boy I think I knew this instinctively and as a result was thoroughly comfortable as a uniformed member of a uniformed organization, though a few years later I was to find the real restrictions of authentic military life oppressive. Scouting was make-believe: I could take it or leave it, as much or as little as I liked and when I chose.

The time I carefully chose to ignore it was the summer, when all aspiring Scouts from throughout that part of North Carolina flocked to Camp Lasater, the official Scout camp a few miles outside Winston-Salem, to surmount the many obstacles they must overcome en route to Eaglehood. All the Speases went there, some many times, as well as numerous other of my good friends, but I avoided it stubbornly. Apart from the emphasis Camp Lasater put on advancement through Scouting ranks, in which I was only dimly and erratically interested, I found the site itself forbidding—the "lake" was muddy and small, it had no canoes and swimming was done not for fun but to teach, predictably life-saving; the tents were damp and overrun with spiders; and the food was said to be inedible. I was a little prig, of course; but I also could scarcely care less about becoming an Eagle Scout and without that goal I sensibly preferred comfort and pleasure.

For me and for most of my friends the principal pleasure of Scouting lay in its dependable companionship and more or less perpetual activity. In the decades before television changed American childhood forever, boys and girls had to find amusement for themselves, and by its stress on the out-of-doors Scouting offered an almost unlimited range of things to do to release the restless energy that all growing boys feel. If you took its rewards for what they were rather than for what they pretended to be, as most of us in Troop 17 did, you could have a wonderful time. Building character was all very well, of course, but fun was better.

It was so much fun, in fact, that we extended it to Sunday afternoons, which were deadly dull anyway. In those days Boy Scout troops were divided into "patrols," which ordinarily meant little. The Beaver Patrol was alive and well, however, thanks to Robert Moore, known universally as "Mo Mo," who was our patrol leader and as indifferent to the nobler aims of Scouting as the rest of us. He and his younger brother Radford lived with their parents in a large, handsome house on a large, handsome lot at the wooded area where Buena Vista blended into the Country Club. Their father, an orthopedic surgeon, was almost as eccentric as Mo Mo, who blinked and twitched and walked with his head aslant and kept his eight or nine minions breathlessly awake wondering what outrageous thing he would do or say next; Mrs. Moore obviously viewed our Sunday meetings in their library with dismay. But we rarely stayed long. Deep woods interspersed with open spaces of red-clay erosion lay just beyond, and after the most perfunctory "meeting" we usually headed there, officially on a "hike." We didn't hike far. Our real destination was the bushy undergrowth within the erosion, which we pulled loose, clay clods and all, and hurled eagerly at one another till the light began to fail. Then we turned homeward, caked with red mud and ecstatically exhausted. That was Scouting for me, for us all—and typical of the Troop 17 spirit—though I don't think Mr. Sebring, the Troop Committee, or, God forgive us, Skipper Vaughan-Lloyd would have approved.

16

Morning Star

Nothing contributed more generously to Winston-Salem's special ambience than the Moravians. Winston's bustle and swank as a successful manufacturing city of the "New South" were attractive and persuasive, and they manifested themselves throughout the business part of town, in the banks and office buildings and in the many fashionable stores lining Fourth Street; but something similar could have been said of a hundred American communities of the sort. Offsetting Winston's air of prosperity, however, were the venerable buildings lining Salem Square, the handsome brick structures of Salem College, Brothers House across the square, the Wachovia Museum, above all Home Moravian Church, which stood like an admonition at the corner and cast its dignity and beauty across everything else; and they were undergirded in their message of stability and order by the rich culture of the Moravians themselves, many of them, most perhaps, descendants of the Moravians who'd settled Salem in the latter years of the eighteenth century. By my time greatly outnumbered by the residents of Winston, not to say surrounded by its swelling geographical expansion, the Moravians remained the nucleus of city life, around which it had been built and against whose strength and purpose it may have measured its own. The Moravians were—as they had been from the beginning—the city's heart, and maybe its soul.

But if different from the Baptists, Methodists, Presbyterians and Episcopalians who were the engine of the city, they were not separate from them. Moravians had been pioneers in raising and selling tobacco, and many old Moravian families were still in the tobacco business, elbow to elbow with the partisans of other denominations; and their role in the city's reputation for craftsmanship was crucial. Socially they were active, for they were, after all, the "old" families of the community; and until a later time Salem College was what the white community could boast of in the realm of higher education. Their hospitality to visitors to their services—and visitors were many, not only from afar but from the city itself—was legendary, the warmth of their denomination everywhere visible and palpable.

The Moravians were industrious, productive and solid, but above all they were calm, as their religion is calm; and this serenity showed itself, to non-Moravians, most characteristically at their two principal observances of the year. No doubt their forebears had brought their deliberate way of doing things with them from Germany and Moravia (part of what is nowadays Czechoslovakia), and clearly their way of marking Christmas and Easter, which were an essential feature of Winston-Salem life for my family and many others, reached North Carolina by the same route. But the Moravians of my youth had changed their Christmas and Easter habits little, and still follow them, in essence, today.

Christmas has become so gaudy a show in our time, so loud and so bright and so secular, that it is difficult to imagine a simpler way of observing it; and it was well on its way to its present dreadful state in the 1930s. But for people in Winston-Salem who wanted to watch its advent and passing more calmly, and for the many visitors from elsewhere who came to Salem seeking the same thing, there were the customs of the Moravians, who decorated their houses only with evergreens and candles at the windows, and who, rather than "celebrate" Christmas with commercial excitement, made it part of their ordinary daily lives.

I cannot remember not going to Salem on Christmas Eve and have pictures in an album somewhere showing me setting out with Mother and Daddy at an early age. The season really began, then and now, with what the Moravians called a "Candle Tea" at Brothers House, though when I was a boy it was not—as it is nowadays, in conjunction with Old Salem's many events—widely announced. You had to know somebody, or call somebody; but Mother knew everybody, and we often went.

Brothers House, where the young single men of the earlier Salem community lived and learned their trades until they married, stood at the principal intersection of Salem Square, a large building three stories above street level and another two, at least, below. You went in from the square, sang Christmas carols in one of the severely beautiful rooms, then went downstairs to watch a display of candlemaking—Moravian Christmas candles are made from a special mixture of beeswax and tallow—and have Moravian coffee and sugar cake; and afterward, as I remember with special vividness, you descended to still another level to see the Christmas Putz, an exquisite table model of Salem in the 1800s, with a crèche, star beaming overhead, at its foot. I thus acquired, not unnaturally, the idea that the nativity had occurred in Salem itself, an idea I have found it hard to modify, let alone correct, in later life. It seemed wonderfully appropriate.

All of this was impressively simple and moving, as were the candles lighted in Salem windows as we came out into the evening darkness; and perhaps it was to show Anne and me that simplicity and quiet were virtues that Mother took us there. She and Daddy were otherwise more or less conventional about Christmas, celebrating it with the usual tree and stockings for Santa Claus to fill, not to mention a Christmas dinner that would have brought a herd of elephants down, all of which they had learned and to which they had become accustomed in their Victorian childhoods. Salem and the simpler customs of the Moravians gave Christmas a firmer foundation.

Moravian bakestuffs were an essential element of the season as well, Moravian Christmas cookies, thin and emitting a gingery spiciness that no non-Moravian ever learned to imitate, as well as Moravian buns; and it was part of the tradition for Mother to take large round tins to West Salem early in December to be filled with freshly baked cookies and buns, within a week or two, by one or the other Moravian women who baked those delicacies at home. But the season reached its climax of particular beauty on Christmas Eve with the Love Feast.

We always went early, Mother being convinced that only by being first in line at the door of Home Moravian Church could we hope to find the seats in the balcony we took year after year. Other families, many non-Moravian, had their own favorite spots, so that going to the Love Feast quickly acquired the ritualistic aspect to which children, unswerving enemies of change from anything they have done more than once, adhere as "tradition." The Rousseaus always sat a row ahead, to our left, the Grays two rows down, to our right, and all around us were the familiar faces of friends and acquaintances, the only change being, from year to year, that everyone looked a little older.

The Love Feast—in fact, there were several, ours being the Children's Love Feast—was a regular Moravian service, but with two important additions. After the singing of carols, the Moravian Band playing just outside, Bishop J. Kenneth Pfohl, head of the southern province of the church, stood and began to tell us the Christmas story. He was an institution as venerable as the buildings of Salem, deep and quavery of voice, and he cast a spell; but after he talked the doors opened and women wearing plain white dresses entered the sanctuary carrying baskets of Moravian buns which they passed down each row of pews. By then our mothers had whipped out the inevitable linen napkins and ordered us, with glares threatening the cessation of Christmas, to put

them on our laps. The buns were followed by trays of hot
Moravian coffee, another delicacy, sweet and milky, that
proved impossible to duplicate at home. That was the simple
meal by which the Moravians commemorated brotherhood
and God's love of man, and there was nothing like it in the
experience of any of us, for it was not a sacrament like Com-
munion and it was wholly free of supernatural overtones or
hocus-pocus; it was simply an act of fellowship, as it seemed.
Then, when the coffee mugs had been collected, the church
suddenly darkened and the doors opened upon the same men
and women bearing trays of lighted Moravian candles, which
they distributed, pew by pew, as before. While they did so
the choir and congregation sang a lovely Moravian carol,
"Morning Star," the choir singing a line, the congregation
repeating it, back and forth through several stanzas; another
anthem was sung antiphonally from the choir loft by Charles
Vance, a tenor who was the father of one of my friends, and
Mrs. Rufus Dalton, the mother of another, and I can never
think of Christmas or the Love Feast without remembering
their high, light voices trading the lines.

The lighting of the church by hundreds of tiny candles in
tiny hands cast another sort of spell, though for the church-
men and the fire department it must have been an ominous
one; and indeed small boys were prone to mischief with
theirs, often wiggling them as signals to one another across
the church. On one memorable occasion someone got too

close to Lila Rousseau, then three or four, and set her long dark locks afire. Adult hands quickly snuffed the flames and no damage resulted, but it was a reminder, if any were needed, that the candles were not without a dangerous side. At a signal from the bishop, finally, all were extinguished and the church lights turned back on; and after a brief prayer we went out and home in the cool December air, our over-excited Christmas spirits turned down for a few moments or hours, our imaginations directed, at least for a little while, toward a side of Christmas we rarely encountered in world-lier Winston. The Love Feast returned Christmas to its place.

The other great Moravian occasion of the year, far more famous beyond Winston-Salem than the Love Feast thanks to its annual broadcast over network radio, was the Easter sun-rise service. This too took place at Home Moravian Church and was as treasured a tradition, but in fact similar services were held, as were similar Love Feasts, at the numerous smaller Moravian churches throughout the old Wachovia area, at Bethabara and Bethania, even older towns than Salem, and at other churches of the denomination that lacked Home Moravian Church's fame.

Bands played a central part in Moravian life generally, and they were an unforgettable element in the Easter service. Begun as "trombone choirs" in an earlier time, but by mine broadened to include other brasses and woodwinds, they played a repertoire of traditional Moravian chorales, carols and hymns, many dating to the eighteenth century, that for sweetness of melody were unrivaled, while the perfect harmonies of brass and woodwind gave them an inimitable sound. The major band had quarters near Salem Square, but it was divided, in turn, into a number of smaller bands; and it was they that woke sleeping Winston-Salem to Easter, moving about the city on trucks borrowed, via Daddy, from Reynolds, stopping, at this corner or that, to play the haunting Moravian chorales against the early morning darkness. Somehow they always seemed to play at our corner of Oaklawn, an arrangement that in later life I realized was not wholly fortuitous. Anne and I came to the window of my room in nightclothes to see them in the cone of yellow light cast by the streetlamp there.

Afterward, near dawn, immense crowds gathered outside the portico at Home Moravian Church, where, precisely at sunup, Bishop Pfohl materialized to pronounce, "The Lord is risen"; whereupon, answering, "The Lord is risen indeed," the vast congregation entered upon a brief liturgy read from a program and accompanied by hymns led by the band. Then the bishop led the worshipers in silence the two or three blocks north of the church to the Moravian graveyard, "God's Acre" as the marker at the entrance called it, where they wound between the rows of freshly scrubbed headstones to a central place where the various bands were gathering and where the final portions of the service were read and answered, the band by then having gathered force and volume from its reassembly. It was typical of Moravian ideas of democracy that the universality of death should be reflected in its burial places: all headstones were flat, white and identical, and—a point that puzzled non-Moravians and outsiders—the dead were buried with their kind, men together, women together, children together, without regard to family affiliation, wealth or class, and in strictly chronological order. But in this there was nothing morbid, as there was nothing showy: death was shown as a fact, freed of sentimental display or ostentation, and this, like so much else in Moravian life, produced an effect of simplicity and great peace. It was also—though no true-blue Moravian would ever have used the word for his church or its ways—a thing of surpassing elegance.

17

Groaning Boards

Food was plentiful and cheap during the '30s, but dining was mostly domestic. The only real restaurants in Winston-Salem—apart from the greasy spoons and all-night cafeterias around the factories—were the dining room and coffee shop at the Robert E. Lee Hotel, where the food was mediocre or worse. Dining out was rare, though the downtown boarding houses flourished. It was necessary to call ahead to be sure the table was not already booked, at least at popular times; but the best of them, like Mrs. Price's on

Spring Street or Mrs. O. G. Allen's on Spruce, were legendary for their fare, which was delicious, abundant and inexpensive. We often ate at one or another of them when Emma was on vacation or had a day off; and though Anne and I hated them, being shy of the strangers we inevitably encountered across the mashed potatoes, they were popular fixtures of Winston-Salem life, surviving well into the 1940s because of their value, conviviality and eminent respectability. Many a bachelor or single schoolteacher dined nowhere else, and the best families in town were regulars.

For the most part, however, we dined at home. The tightness and compactness of family life as the Victorians had ordained it was still the social norm, and taking meals together was its most characteristic manifestation. Besides, dinner was the only time of day on weekdays when we were all home together—though we called it "supper" unless there was company or we were talking about the midday meal Sunday, when by unspoken understanding "supper" and "lunch" became "dinner"—and the result was that supper became the focal point of family life. The day's activities were reported and its disasters bemoaned, and Mother invariably took advantage of the occasion—since the evening meal was ritual as well as nourishment—to urge uplift, especially if, as was frequently the case, I was in another of my self-indulgent phases and had grown lax with my schoolwork. Enjoying my many advantages, I had a duty to do my best, she invariably

reminded me, failing to explain, however, what I came gradually to realize, that in her eyes anything but straight-A work
leading to Phi Beta Kappa and a Nobel Prize was less than
my best. Like most boys exposed to counsels of improvement
I soon learned to let the evening homily pass without dispute,
though the ultimate effect was ironically not so much to elevate my own accomplishment as to make me all too critical,
like her, of the shortcomings of others.

The main event of the hour was not the pursuit of my
perfection, however, but general conversation, which was
lively and varied and into which everyone was drawn, children, guests, occasionally even Emma as she circled the big
round table serving this course or that. Everything human
beings could do or think about, with an obvious exception or
two, was discussable and, sooner or later, discussed. Far from
being banned at the table, religion and politics got the most
attention, though books, music, sports, relatives, town gossip
and the toll the Depression was taking on American spirits
came up again and again; and though my parents were determined that Anne and I should acquire manners suitable to
the eighteenth century, or at any rate the antebellum South,
they also encouraged us to pile into the talk—no nonsense,
for them, about our being seen and not heard. They had
strong opinions themselves on everything, especially Mother,
who was, after all, a McDowell, and they liked strong opinions in others, thought it an American's duty to form and

express them; and they expected us to form opinions too and to learn at an early age to defend or modify them. By disposition milder, Daddy generally let Mother frame whatever issue came up; but then, having heard this side and that, he liked to pounce, and his conclusions, often stated with epigrammatical pith, could be both wise and witty—as when, of the rumor that one of his political heroes was again pondering a presidential run, he suggested it was really "McAdoo about nothing." I was so like Mother emotionally that I frequently plunged in before I thought, but both of them always heard me out patiently and attentively. My heated opinion, offered at eight or nine during a discussion of the New Deal and taxes, that I'd "never have children: they cost too much and are just a nuisance anyway" became a staple of family folklore. It also proved to be a poor prediction.

The food on the table, constantly replenished by Emma, was plentiful but by today's standards probably monotonous. Frozen foods of any sort lay in the future, as did the national mania for steak set off by World War II, and grocery stores offered a far more limited range of choices than today's supermarkets. Fresh fish or seafood were available only irregularly from the stalls of downtown's city market, and in the absence of large-scale interstate trucking, so essential to modern food marketing, fresh produce was limited, except on special occasions, to what farms of the immediate region could offer. Mostly Mother and Emma bought fresh vegetables and fruit off the little truck, complete with a scale hanging at the rear, brought a couple of times a week to the front of the driveway by a farmer and his sons, all of whom answered to "Mr. Conrad," but they had to content themselves with whatever Mr. Conrad and the Basketeria between them had to offer. Often it was not much and never was it as varied as supermarkets of a later time routinely carried.

The Basketeria was an institution eliminated, like most of its fellows all over America, by postwar food chains and shopping malls, the small neighborhood grocery patronized almost exclusively by the residents of a particular part of town. Actually, Buena Vista being ruthlessly residential, it was not in the neighborhood at all, but in a clump of small businesses on the edge of Hanes Park at the foot of Summit Street hill; but, like the drugstore, the barber shop, filling station, Dr. Pepper bottling works and two small Greek restaurants arrayed alongside, it had a neighborhood air. The Basketeria itself catered so narrowly to the affluent families of Buena Vista and Reynolda that casual shoppers might have found it unfriendly. A clerk waited on customers, alone handling the cans, boxes and wrapped packets of meat or produce, and a stock boy bagged them for house delivery by the Basketeria truck; patrons were not encouraged to handle merchandise. Much of the time, moreover, customers like Mother shopped by telephone, conferring each morning with the indispensable Miss McBride, who advised as to availability, freshness and quality before taking the order, which in due course, often within minutes, was delivered down the driveway, through the back porch and onto the kitchen table by a tall, skinny, blond young man; and he often made a second delivery in the late afternoon of this can or that bag forgotten or overlooked by Mother or Emma that morning. Such service was taken for granted. Miss McBride sometimes initiated it herself, ringing back to report what a wholesaler had just brought in that we might want for supper.

Supper was nonetheless predictable: limited choice led to limited cuisine, which was quintessentially Southern as well. Each summer Daddy contracted for a dozen hams from Mr. Kern, in Fincastle, and when they came along in the fall he hung them systematically from overhead hooks above the basement stairs, then carefully prepared them himself, with sugar, molasses, pepper and cloves, as they were brought up, one by one through the winter and spring, for Emma to cook; like many Virginians he and Mother believed that nothing but the Presbyterian Church and the Democratic Party were better than a Virginia ham, with the result that we ate a great deal of it, taking special delight at the surgical finesse with which Daddy carved it in long, thin slices of a rich brown hue. A roasted chicken graced the table Sundays, of course, and now and then we had a roast or pot roast; turkeys were reserved for Thanksgiving and Christmas, lamb for Easter, and the only kinds of steak we knew were country and Swiss. All of this was accompanied by an abundance of vegetables, green peas and string and lima beans, baked, creamed, scalloped and sweet potatoes, creamed onions, spinach, turnip greens, mustard and kale; but except in spring and summer much of it was necessarily canned, though Irish and sweet potatoes were bought in bulk and stored away in a dry bin belowstairs. Those were the years of the Depression, however, and though we were among the lucky ones, expensive foods were avoided and wasting food condemned, besides which Mother, prompted by a loathing of finickiness created by the stubborn unwillingness of her father and brothers to swallow more than a dab of this and a taste of that (my grandfather would request "one pea, please"), was determined that Anne and I should eat everything set before us— and we did, too, Anne protesting with world-class tenacity but inevitably, being no match for Mother, taking the hated bite. In time she and I learned to like cabbage, broccoli, Brussels sprouts and what seems in retrospect an endless tidal wave of macaroni and cheese. Okra defeated me till I was grown, however, when I realized with regret how many pods I'd quietly, and successfully, stuffed in my pockets.

The glory of the food, in any case, was Emma's cooking. She was an instinctively gifted cook, a natural, and once they'd discovered her skill Mother's friends were forever borrowing her for their parties or asking her to fix them some special delicacy. The truth was, however—or so both always claimed—that she'd arrived on our doorstep from low-country South Carolina unable to cook at all and that Mother's instruction and recipes were the true secret of her prowess. Perhaps that was true, or partly true; but though Mother could indeed, if she had to, perform in the kitchen, and always could do a few choice dishes better, when Emma left us for factory work a few months after Pearl Harbor, to return only on special occasions, we began going out for supper a great deal—and Mother confessed herself that her "hand was out."

Sumptuous as our suppers and Sunday dinners often were, lunch on Saturday quickly became the favorite meal of the week. That may have had the simple explanation that Saturday was a day free of school and the limp, pallid lunches, whether out of a brown paper bag or in the school lunchroom, that remain more than half a century later a grisly memory; but I expect we loved Saturday lunch because it was different from any other meal of the week. Many of Daddy's men at the Reynolds garage lived in the country outside Winston-Salem, which was still geographically small, and most of them maintained small farms in which they grew most of their own produce and raised chickens and hogs for their own tables. Many hunted regularly as well. The result was that week after week they brought him the bounty of their efforts: spareribs, sauerkraut their wives had made, sausage and fresh country bacon at hog-killing time, pheasant and squab. Anne was a partisan of the latter, which she called "squabbies," and Emma roasted them with her usual skill, though biting down on a few shot here and there could be startling. Spareribs were a greater delicacy than she or I realized, but they were deliciously different from the lettuce-and-tomato sandwiches, long since soaked through with mayonnaise, that were our usual school-day fare. Mother often made a huge vat of vegetable soup or Brunswick stew Saturday morning, and sometimes she and Emma worked up a batter she poured into the old round waffle iron at one end of the breakfast-room table. Black-bottom pie, another of Anne's favorites, usually appeared as if by magic.

Most of our food was Southern and simple, modest by the gastronomic standards of a later time, but Emma had mastered nearly all of it when I began to notice what I was eating: all sorts and kinds of meat and fish, all the vegetables, and with an unusual lightness, as well as a taste for flavors, I have rarely found elsewhere. She took roasts out of the oven before they fell apart, stopped vegetables before they got mushy; her sauces were zestful but never heavy; and she seemed to have a particular knack for baking, always fixing fresh rolls for supper, sometimes spoonbread or Sally Lunn, and was sure to see to it that a cake or pie or tin of raisin cookies was on the breakfast-room sideboard for late-afternoon or bedtime snacks. Her triumph, though, was her rusk, which she baked regularly, small sweet rolls glazed on top with butter and sugar; everyone, especially Mother's friends, loved them, and when we went to my grandparents' in Fincastle in the summer, where by universal demand Emma took charge of the bread, her rusk reached even greater popularity and was one of the few things I ever saw my grandfather eat with enthusiasm. In later years, when I was in my teens, she routinely baked me latticework apple and blackberry pies that I just as routinely took to my room and washed down, in a single solitary sitting, with a quart of cold milk. She also did most of the laundry, all of the housecleaning, and babysat Anne, Lila and me for six dollars a week and a garage room heated only by a woodstove, with Thursday and Sunday afternoons off. We took it all, and her, perfectly for granted.

18

Hard Times

<u>——————</u>

I remember my boyhood as a time of unbroken sunshine, but this is only one of the many tricks of memory by which we reshape the past to satisfy our dreams of a Golden Age. The overriding and unmistakable fact of the '30s was the Depression, nowadays a fading image of closed factories and men in bread lines. For my parents and members of their generation, utterly innocent of economics and of any political reality beyond their own benign, Jeffersonian democracy, it was inconceivable and thus for a long time impossible. Their faith in the stability of the world they knew, bolstered by the sweetness of small-town life at the turn of the century and left unshaken by their brief experience of the World War, made it hard for them to acknowledge the visible collapse of the American system, let alone the broader truth that this collapse was worldwide and could end by destroying the order, progress, dependability and good will they believed to be the essential features of "civilization." That it nearly did so by encouraging the rise of European totalitarianism they only recognized, like most Americans, slowly and belatedly; for it was a corollary of their confidence in the indestructibility of their country's institutions that they believed the right political leader, Franklin Delano Roosevelt, with the properly energetic program, the New Deal, could soon restore the old, safe, above all comprehensible society in which they had lodged so much reliance. No doubt, too, that trust proved, for a time, self-fulfilling. The Depression was a mistake; it would be corrected by reason.

Whatever its causes or cures, in any case, it was visibly, inescapably there; not even the comfortable insularity of Buena Vista could conceal from its residents the devastation it was wreaking. The front pages of the *Journal* and *Sentinel* provided a daily toll of horror in the industrial northeast and midwest, in the drought-stricken farmlands of the Dust Bowl; pictures of bread lines and the pinched faces of the starving in the great cities provided grim visualization of the nightly *guignol* described on radio, while to all of them the frequent "fireside chats" of FDR were a warm but somehow sinister counterpoint—to need comfort was to realize, after all, that some disaster had occurred for which one required comfort. Winston-Salem suffered far less unemployment than most industrial cities, especially Southern textile cities—people reassured themselves with the cliché that the smoking of cigarettes, the community's economic foundation, actually increased in bad times—and the sight of bread lines, soup kitchens and failed businesses was unknown downtown; but the ambitious "skyscraper" Van Dyck Building, put up about the time of the Crash on a prominent corner facing Courthouse Square, stood mostly empty above the ground for most of the decade, and the large department store scheduled to fill most of its floors languished and closed after a year or two. Men peddling pencils stood at many a street corner, and all of us, even if our fathers had good, secure jobs, grew accustomed to hand-me-downs.

But the detail I remember most vividly was at home: the sight of sometimes as many as a dozen out-of-work men who'd crisscrossed the country in the futile pursuit of work eating Saturday lunch on our back porch steps, led to our door by word of mouth and the chalk marks by which they blazed their trails to houses known to be hospitable. Now and then Daddy was able to put one or two to work for a few hours in the yard; but not often, for three of the black men from his own crew at Reynolds depended on their Saturday wages from him—Jim and Henry and Will, all of whom became friends of mine—and he felt obligated to use them as often as he could. It was understood throughout the mid-thirties, however, that Emma made plenty of extra lunch on Saturdays, spareribs and boiled potatoes and cabbage and string beans, for the nomadic unemployed in case they turned up. I often talked with them as they ate, decent, well-spoken men desperately down on their luck, and more than one told me he had a boy my age back home in Pennsylvania or Indiana. The occasional realization that, had his luck been different, my father could be a hobo too brought tears to my eyes.

Another Depression memory is of empty rooms in virtually empty houses. From my earliest years my parents encouraged me to make my range of friendships broader than the safe little island of Buena Vista afforded, and once I was in school I began to do so. My friends in the neighborhood remained my closest, the Speas boys, Grady, Sonny when he was well enough, but school soon opened up other possibilities and reinforced my parents' point: that the world was large and varied and that I could learn and benefit from that variety. Wiley School was not only strong but a melting pot, drawing heavily from three-year or four-year schools all over central Winston-Salem. Its students—always excepting the fact that all of them were white—represented a cross section of city life: poor boys from the factory village wearing tattered overalls and carrying huge chips on their shoulders; the sons and daughters of downtown shopkeepers or service workers, carpenters and electricians and plumbers and mechanics, often nearly threadbare too but most of them bright and ambitious and confident in themselves as the factory children were not; my first Jewish friends—Marty Levin, a mischievous imp even smaller than I, who stood up to playground bullies and took a bad licking for it more than once; Shevel Siff, who became a partner in my touring marionette show; and Harriet Cohen, who came over from West End in Miss Richard's fifth grade and soon established herself as the quickest student in what was already supposed to be a fast class. At my mother's behest Harriet became the first girl I had a date with, driven solemnly, silently by Daddy to a concert; he told me years afterward I never said a word. She and I became lifelong friends who still see each other from time to time, joined no doubt to eternity by the single occasion in history on which I was speechless.

None of them lived in empty rooms or empty houses, but I knew others who did. One asked me home after school one day and on the long walk through Hanes Park and up Broad Street hill told me his father was out of work. I don't suppose I yet quite grasped what that meant, for when we reached his house, a big frame bungalow in a perfectly respectable neighborhood, I was shocked to see a yard worn down to the dirt from neglect and, inside, nothing but space.

There were no rugs on the floors. There were no curtains at the windows or pictures on the walls. A single bookcase built beneath the front window of the living room stood empty. The only furniture to be seen was in the kitchen, where a battered table and a couple of chairs occupied the center of the room, and in my friend's room, where he had an old iron bed—his clothes were stacked on a footlocker he told me had been his father's in the World War. No doubt his parents had a bed too, perhaps even a chest of drawers, but I never saw them. The house was as barren of life as it was of objects—there was, of course, no car in driveway or garage—and was as cold as the tomb it resembled. We played an invented version of hockey, with rulers and a ball of tablet paper, on the gleaming floor of the dining room in which, it was obvious, no one ever dined.

Eventually I realized I had a lot of school friends living like that: families of the office-working or tradesman middle class whose livelihoods and thus whose lives had been abruptly taken from them. They had no way of surviving from week to week beyond the wages they brought home on payday. Most came from country families as hard hit as they. No public assistance was available to the unemployed, no aid for dependent children, no food stamps. Women like my friend's mother sometimes could pick up a little money as seamstresses or baking cakes or Moravian food near Christmas, but it was only change; and—ironically, in so segregated a society—jobs as cooks and housekeepers and laundresses were jealously reserved for black women, and the willingness of white women to take them or their attempts to get them were widely resented by blacks and fortunate whites alike. All of this slowly abated as the '30s passed and the New Deal and the "natural forces of recovery" worked their uncertain wonders; but the scars left by the Depression on its victims were permanent, as were its memories on the luckier of us. Frugality became reflexive, fearing the worst habitual.

Against that darkness our house cast a little circle of light and warmth, and so I remember it: Mother at the piano, playing songs from old Broadway musical comedies and operettas I'd come to love from her stacks of sheet music, Jolson's "Mammy," "Madrigal of May" from the Barrymores' *Jest*, Jerome Kern's "Look for the Silver Lining," the cover adorned with Marilyn Miller and Leon Errol; Daddy at the card table, legal pad and a sheaf of papers before him, working on Mrs. J. B. Dyer's income taxes; Anne silently playing endless hands of solitaire on the floor beside him. The calamities of the Depression seemed, those evenings, to belong to some other world.

19

The Joys and Woes of Capitalism

By a paradox of the sort that delights the philo-
sophical, boys of my generation were encouraged to work but
forbidden to do so. What sociologists of the future would
identify as the Puritan work ethic was in full sway. Even well-
to-do parents took it for granted that their sons would benefit from work by acquiring a respect for industry and discipline and developing a sense of the worth of earned money.
But the reality of the Depression made even the simplest job

too valuable to offer to anyone less than a man who headed a household. The result was a quandary obvious to every growing boy urged to learn what the adult world was like: even if he wanted to work there was little work to be had.

There were exceptions to the general dearth of part-time jobs, of course. A few of my friends found regular places filling grocery bags on Saturday afternoons. Every August Reynolds opened the leaf house for a few weeks to the sons of its executives and their friends during the season when Georgia tobacco came in from the markets down south; the leaves, piled onto huge burlap squares tied by the corners, had to be shaken of their dirt and dust before going to the stemmer and more elaborate stages of storage and manufacture, a dirty task few of us liked. There were jobs jerking sodas at drugstore fountains, and a few drugstores offering curb service employed boys to wait cars as well. But most work—if for pay—was made up: raking your father's leaves or mowing his grass, washing his car, selling magazines like *Liberty* or the *Saturday Evening Post* door-to-door on weekends. The fast-food chains had yet to be invented and waiting restaurant tables was difficult when there were few restaurants. My most industrious friend, Tommy Speas, found a spot selling produce at a little market on Courthouse Square, but he had to pester the owner to death to get it.

In summers, however, there was the drink stand. Livingston Johnson, son of one of Winston-Salem's most prominent physicians, had one for years on the empty corner lot next to his family's house, and it quickly became the place where boys of Buena Vista hung out from June to September, their bicycles littering the mud ruts that soon developed around the stand. Grady and I determined to go into the same business ourselves, and with my parents' encouragement we soon were flourishing on the strip of grass between the Oaklawn Avenue sidewalk and street. The stand itself, luckily for us, did not have to be built from scratch: Daddy called a bottler who knew a boy who'd run a stand the year before, and what with this and that and probably a dollar or two, we acquired it, a sturdy thing of two-by-fours covered with the tin signs of the soft drinks we proposed to carry: Coca-Cola, Pepsi-Cola, Double Cola, Royal Crown Cola, Nehi and so forth. The next thing to find was a cooler to hold drinks and ice, and Daddy found that too. Then the work began.

The work consisted of, first, getting up in the morning, which was not as easy as it sounded, and getting out to the stand; second, buying the day's ice when the ice truck arrived. I was a poor financier and Grady was worse, if possible, and finding the necessary cash from the previous day's proceeds took ingenuity. By then the morning had grown warm and patrons were beginning to gather by the curb. Mostly these were friends, however, all wanting a drink on credit, which neither of us was good at either refusing or remembering. By mid-morning the drink trucks were arriving too to sell us the day's bottles, which had to be paid for, of course, with cash. The idea was that we bought at wholesale, sold at retail, which in the case of soft drinks at that time meant buying for four cents and selling for a nickel. This was called free enterprise.

I am sorry to say that we did poorly at it. Besides keeping pale accounts of our extensions of credit, we never seemed to know how much cash we had and rarely bought drinks in the proper quantities, which both of us were too worthless to calculate. Grady did the noontime swing of building sites in the neighborhood, selling a few bottles to carpenters from his wretchedly decrepit bicycle; and I tried to scare up sales to servants or salesmen passing on the sidewalk or waiting for the bus across the street. Our greatest failures were failures of character, however. The broiling sun of early afternoon heated the stand so much it melted the ice in the cooler, which meant that late-afternoon drinks invariably were warm, though by then, having closed down for an hour or two to play tennis, we were rarely able to find customers anyway. Worse, we drank up whatever potential profits we might have anticipated: Grady almost always had gone through the chocolate milk by noon, and I was equally piggy with the Pepsis. Our fathers shook their heads but did not fuss. Mother allowed the destruction to her grass, which was total, to pass without complaint, supposing it would regrow next year and that summer occupation was more important anyhow. By the end of August Daddy and Mr. Southern figured we'd lost about a dollar and a half since June.

But the most valuable job a boy could have—it was like owning a tract of business property in downtown Los Angeles—was carrying papers. A paper route not only made a little money every week, it was a source of power and prestige, and everybody wanted one. They were not easy to come by, however. The system by which newspapers all over England and America did their local distribution had been finely honed by the English "penny press" a century before. In monopoly newspaper cities like Winston-Salem—by then the norm all over America—the owners of papers were free to concentrate on good service to their customers; the need to sell their product competitively was small, there being no competition. In Winston-Salem this meant that the same company published both morning paper, the *Journal*, and evening paper, the *Twin City Sentinel*, as well as a combined Sunday edition called the *Journal and Sentinel*, and could control without argument the circulation of them all. This meant, in turn, that they could pick and choose which boys got what routes.

You ordinarily waited years to get a route and spent most of them working toward it. Chattel slavery had been ended legally by the Civil War, but boys are good at evading legal niceties and the newspaper circulation office helped them out. A succession of older boys—Roland Richmond, Jimmy

Hancock, Bill Williamson, his younger brother Dan—had carried Oaklawn Avenue, and each had served a time of indentured apprenticeship to his predecessor before he gained possession. I came at the end of that line and, during my last year of high school, took a slave of my own into camp.

The heart of the system was that the *Journal* and *Sentinel* would allow only one boy to carry both papers. This was lucrative—or lucrative by the standards of the time—but wearing: it meant six morning runs, six evening runs, a Sunday run and a run, the hardest task of all, to collect the week's take, plus a Saturday-afternoon trip downtown to pay the bill. A boy who had a route characteristically did them all his first year, then found a younger boy thereafter to carry either the morning or evening run, usually—the early-morning hours being cold—the former. The understanding was that the apprentice eventually got the route.

I got it from Dan Williamson by that means, carrying his afternoon papers during the fall, when he played football, his morning papers in the spring and summer, when he wanted to sleep. It was hard but fair, and even efficient in a way: by the time I took over the route I knew every house, dog and deadbeat on it, and had made a dollar a week doing it. The transfer of ownership was rarely less than successful. Dan, finally tiring of it, let me have it because I had worked for it, because I knew what I was doing without having to be taught and because Mr. Lindsay, the man downtown who ran the newsboys' routes, would accept me.

It took more work than many boys would happily have undertaken, however. You had to get up about five, something a sleepy growing boy finds hard to do, dress in the cold, then walk half a mile to the Sherrills' house on Carolina Circle to pick up your papers from the stack of bundles dropped there, if you were lucky, a few minutes earlier. You unwrapped the copper wire and counted them to be sure you were not short. Then, putting them in the big canvas bag bought from the newspaper, you set out to start your route, rolling the papers into throwable tubes as you went, something you had to keep doing the rest of the run. The morning air could be biting and yards were pitch-black, so that you had to know your way through the bushes if you were to take the innumerable shortcuts all of us found. Dogs were plentiful, some mean, and invariably one or two customers would be up and waiting before you got to them. One of mine, the treasurer of the Reynolds Tobacco Company, was curt and unfriendly and had a vicious Great Dane to boot. I never satisfied him, and more than once his dog mangled the paper before he got it. This was my fault too.

You were back in bed by six or a little after, to catch another hour of sleep before school; but then the whole thing began again that afternoon around four, except that some people who took the *Journal* did not take the *Sentinel* while some who took the *Sentinel* did not take the *Journal*, which meant keeping your shifts straight; and both got Sunday papers, which were heavy to carry and usually required two runs, a task in which Anne often assisted, not necessarily in good spirit. The worst job was collecting, and no one could do that for you. The system—to avoid child-labor problems—was built on the fiction that the newspaper "sold" its product to "independent" carriers, who then resold them to their customers; the boy got his bill with his Friday afternoon papers and paid it next day. The system did not mention, of course, that it rigidly controlled the carriers by picking them carefully and requiring a bond, as well as pulling their routes if they proved to be unsatisfactory.

"Collecting" was more difficult than it should have been because people are glad to get their papers but unhappy about having to pay for them. Often they couldn't find the cash, even in prosperous Buena Vista, or offered payment in a bill too large for me to change. Some, of odious memory, hid when I rang the doorbell, eventually running up enormous bills because I had paid for their papers for weeks. Others forgot whether they paid me or at the office; this had the wonderful result, in one case, that a Winston-Salem judge on my route, whose paper I carried for years, ran into Daddy and asked him why I hadn't collected from him lately; I'd had him on my books as an "office pay," which meant that I was supposed to be credited for my profit, when in fact he was not. The payoff, which he made with a flourish, was terrific. Others were less benign, and it often took me two or three trips a weekend to get them to pay. But I had to pay by five Saturday, and ruined more than one Saturday afternoon making the rounds redundantly.

Still, it was the best job I ever had, man or boy, and I remember it with warm gratitude. Though I was a poor businessman, I managed to keep a reasonably orderly account book. Though indirectly I worked for the paper, Mr. Lindsay rarely gave me grief and I had the illusion, which the system encouraged, of immense independence. I got to know every family on my street and learned to like almost all of them. The work gave me exercise and kept me out of doors. Now and then a younger woman would flirt with me when I came to collect, never seriously and never dangerously, and that was good for my pubescent ego. Finally, there was all that money: a good week made me six dollars, sometimes seven, and I could always count on clearing four. I may have failed to learn thrift, but I was a capitalist.

20

The Groves of Academe

On a cold January night in 1938, scarcely weighing a hundred pounds and only a whisper above five feet tall, I graduated from Calvin H. Wiley School, set at last upon the vast and often frightening adventure of high school. I was still short of thirteen and had been in elementary school less than the nominal seven years, but by a fluke in the North Carolina educational system I was deemed ready for the higher learning: since children in those days "skipped" half a grade or even a grade, I and virtually all of my first-grade classmates from Miss Wilson's room had made an early jump in our advancement, the first half of the second grade, and now found ourselves in the irregular position of graduating half a year off the ordinary cycle. This was a routine occurrence, however; to return us to our slot in normal phase our parents contrived, with the open connivance of the system, for us to drop a required course somewhere along the way, necessitating an additional semester in high school. The result was that we spent six and a half years in elementary school, four and a half in high, which was as absurd as it sounds.

I remember little of commencement night, which took place, with appropriate pomp, in the Wiley School auditorium. I wore long pants for the first time—till then, like most of my friends except the lankiest, I'd worn either shorts or knickers—and, another first, a real shirt with a real collar and a real necktie; widespread collars, like Shelley's, and shorter ties were the custom for small boys. I gave the welcoming address, for reasons I neither understood nor liked, and immediately forgot the rest of the evening altogether.

By then, the relative brevity of my stay notwithstanding, I knew Wiley inside out and had mastered its darkest secrets. I knew the best spots on the immense Hanes Park playground to take my brown-bag lunch in peace; I knew the best places on the bank of Peters Creek to wade in (and once, in the second grade, to fall into, a rite of passage through which all boys were expected to pass); I knew how to avoid hall monitors and the roughneck boys of Chatham Heights, who could trounce any of us Buena Vista boys without dirtying their hands; and I knew which were the best times to go to the library, and with whom, to study the little blue books, purchased behind O'Hanlon's drugstore downtown, that showed prominent comic-strip heroes and heroines in steamy, if richly plagiarized, fornication. In turn I'd been taught by Miss Edwards, Miss Richard, Miss Matlock, Miss Crichton, Miss Hudson and Miss Maggie Rierson, whose specialty was movies about North Carolina that always broke in mid-reel; and I'd had music from Miss Obenshain, who was a Virginia friend of my parents, and art from Miss Newton, whose first name was Fiona and who encouraged me to paint. I liked all of them except Miss Matlock, who though an excellent pedagogue got my number from the first and bullied me unmercifully to do neater work; and in Miss Mattie Richard I had the best teacher, my mother apart, of my life.

One of my many avocational interests throughout my Wiley years, inspired by the touring company of Tony Sarg, was marionettes. From books and seeing his plays I knew that true marionettes had to be hinged at the joints and operated accordingly, but that was beyond my limited carpentry; instead I drew figures on a sheet of corrugated cardboard and cut them out with a jackknife, then colored them with crayons and watercolors and wired them up by attaching long threads through the shoulders to wood chips that served as hand controls. Daddy obligingly found a large cardboard packing box and cut out a proscenium and stage on one side; I then colored them and added, with Mother's help, a curtain I could roll up and down from behind the arch. It was inelegant, to put it mildly, and the characters wobbled and danced rather than moving in imitation of human movement; but it was a show and all of us loved it, Tommy and Harriet and Shevel and I taking it all over Wiley, at the request of teachers who'd heard of it and wanted something to amuse their charges. I wrote the plays, which were mostly imitations of the Jack Benny Sunday night radio program, and we performed them happily and without self-consciousness of any sort, confident that the theatrical illusions we created ranked with Tony Sarg's.

Shows like his came to school regularly and were, in fact, the only true stagecraft we saw except for the annual Junior League children's play and the Saturday afternoon stage shows at the State. Magicians were a regular fixture, some good, some less so, and they spawned in turn a variety of homegrown magicians of high-school age; the best of them called himself Ashburn the Magician and swept onstage in a black cape that he mysteriously wrapped around himself at dramatic moments, though to believe in him we had to forget for a few minutes that he was only Anderson Ashburn, who lived over on First Street somewhere and was just a few years ahead of us in school. Charles Speas, who ordered his tricks from Johnson-Smith and always forgot what he was supposed to do at the crucial moment, was the worst. Every spring brought a team of Filipino yo-yo stars, who did amazing stunts and sold yo-yos afterward from a stall at Woolworth's; and there were numerous animal acts, probably old circus or vaudeville acts, now reduced to touring schools with their dogs that ran basketballs and jumped hoops.

By 1938, though of modest physical dimensions and as scruffy as a twelve-year-old boy can be, I had been in love again and again. My romances were entirely imaginary and starkly chaste even so, since sex was something we knew nothing about beyond what we saw in the little blue books and rigidly disassociated from real life. I had little respect for girls, being a wholly conventional subscriber to all *macho* ideas, but I sensed this was inadequate to the real world, in which women like Mother functioned with verve and wisdom and girls like my friends in school invariably did better work than any boy in class; besides, I liked them. Sooner or later I fell hopelessly in love with them all, though this did nothing to affect my daily life and rarely bothered my pursuit of my interests. Boys were accustomed to writing their girls' initials on their palms in the ink that was then used in the penmanship classes, and at one point I encountered a crisis when I fell in love with so rapid a succession of girls in one week that I had trouble erasing one set of letters to make room for the next; but I solved the matter when I realized that, since all of them had first names beginning with "J," I need only rub out the second initial. Jean Stockton, June Thomasson, Jean Shoemaker: little did they guess the throes of passion into which they had plunged me.

My destination after Wiley was R. J. Reynolds High School, which lay just across Northwest Boulevard and up a steep slope of pine forest on a hilltop connected to Hanes Park by a tunnel. Legend had it that all manner of dire tragedies awaited incoming freshmen there, but I knew better because I had been there often. In the seventh grade, again for reasons unknown to me, I'd been named editor-in-chief of the *Wiley Post*, the school newspaper; my duties were mysterious, since I never edited anything and apart from writing a pompous editorial for each issue never saw the rest of the copy, but one chore I was given was to carry the contents for the paper up the hill to Reynolds, where it would be set in type and printed by the boys in the Reynolds printing program. Among the glories of Reynolds's curriculum were fully fleshed industrial arts sequences in woodwork, machine-shop technology and printing, and Mr. Elrick's print shop, though relatively small, was equipped with everything from a bank of linotypes and a Ludlow typograph to a flatbed press that did all the school's printing, including its yearbook, as well as odd jobs like the *Wiley Post*. Most of its graduates went on into the printing trades, and when I went to work as a reporter for the *Winston-Salem Journal* more than a decade later I encountered the same faces in the composing room I'd known years earlier at Reynolds.

It was almost universally acknowledged to be, in any case the finest high school in North Carolina, perhaps in the South; an apocryphal story held that a prominent Winston-Salem businessman who could have afforded to send his boys anywhere was warned by the headmaster of a famous Virginia prep school that though he'd be happy to have them, "Your sons cannot get a better education than Reynolds High School provides."

The school itself, built alongside Reynolds Auditorium (which served both city and high school) in the early 1920s, was three stories high around two inner courtyards that were supposed to serve as botanical gardens but never did. The classrooms were large and light, illuminated either by the courtyards or the hilltop sky. Careful planning had placed departments in convenient combinations. The home economics department on the lower level took sewing room and kitchen to the corner where the school kitchen started. The business department above it had rooms for typing and bookkeeping. There were rooms for mechanical drawing, a separate space in the auditorium wing for music and band, a journalism newsroom around the corner from the print shop where Mrs. Swaim's classes produced the Reynolds newspaper and yearbook, a fine library near the center of the building and, along the west wall, a three-story science wing, with classrooms and laboratories for general science, biology, chemistry and physics, all with equipment and work benches superior to what I found when I entered college. The print shop occupied one ground-floor corner and the other shops had sturdy buildings on the grounds. But the feature of Reynolds that no one who ever attended it ever forgot was a row of animal heads, a rhino and a hippo, a lion and a tiger, as well as numerous exotic deer and bison, given the school by a local tycoon who'd bagged them on a safari through Africa and, after mounting them, had nowhere his wife would let him show them. They stood in ominous symbolic warning along the wall beside the principal's office, a silent reminder of the fate awaiting all miscreants.

Discipline was said to be stern at Reynolds, and in academic life it was; but I rarely encountered anything rougher than a frown otherwise. Miss Ethel Ervin, by whom I was introduced to Latin, was a fine scholar and dedicated teacher whose drills were incessant. Miss Sarah Olive Smith, who headed the math department, taught me algebra, plain and solid geometry and trigonometry between her legendary wheezing chuckles, whipping string and chalk through the air to draw her illustrative circles on the blackboard. Miss Kathryn Emmart let me dissect a cat while I was taking her second-year biology course, and W. S. Buchanan took me on as his lab assistant in chemistry when I was a senior. The richest legends of all were those surrounding Miss Mary Wiley, who taught only senior English and only on her own eccentric terms; she was the daughter of the man who'd founded the school system and for whom Wiley School was named, and she gave no quarter to anyone, official or unofficial, who tried to alter her teaching methods. Her concentration invariably fell on her senior homeroom class, whose members she picked and whose minds she then proceeded to control by a series of surprises—she liked to have the class abruptly rise and be assigned new seats, which she chose in order of merit—that kept everyone in a state of suspense and strict attention. You had to answer to the name she gave you, too, which was often bewildering: she'd taught many of our parents and insisted on calling us them.

Most of that lay ahead of me in the spring of 1938, however. I was a tiny freshman trying hard to be a teenager, which seemed to me an infinitely desirable but difficult thing to become. I was interested in girls. I was interested in chemistry and baseball. But more than anything else I was interested in tennis, in the mastery of which I knew my destiny must surely lie. One late March day I thus decided to go out for a place on the tennis team, then dominated by such stars as Moyer and Roger Hendrix, Bob and John Haltiwanger, Bob McCuiston and Jimmy Hancock, Berk Ingram and Hartsell Cash, all a few years older, not to say far better players, than I. But I was undaunted. I found a pair of white shorts and white sneakers and—because I knew from newspaper photos that Bill Tilden and Fred Perry always came on court wearing sleeveless sweaters—an old, fuzzy, green one from the floor of my closet; and, thus costumed, I presented myself at Hanes Park courtside. Coach Walker Barnette, eventually to become a dear friend, looked up, gave his cigar a thoughtful chew and, turning to his regulars, said, "My God, what's this?"

21
Dames

Though always in love I had no idea that love and sex were associated. Bob Whaling, a new boy in the neighborhood, was a year or two older and richly more salacious than I, but the things he told me about sex struck my pubescent ears as so preposterous I rejected them out of hand; and by the time I realized that some of them were true I had passed into the helplessness of adolescence and was thus of no danger to anyone, especially myself.

I was free, as a result, to moon away to my heart's content over the endless parade of pretty girls who passed through my daydreaming life. It was no triumph of mine that they were there, however; my adoration of them was wholly silent, even sullen, because I was afraid of them, the prettier the worse, and like most of my friends went to great lengths to avoid actually talking with them, let alone taking them to the movies or buying them a soda at the drugstore. I understood perfectly, from observing their inevitably superior perform- ance in school, that girls were trouble—the movies and boys' books on which I doted said so, after all, and the danger they exuded as they passed was palpable. I did not, of course, count the girls I had been friends with since the first grade as girls; they were pals, and could always be counted on to explain the mysteries of multiplication. Real girls—the pretty girls I fell in love with daily—were in some other homeroom. A possible exception was Jean Stockton, who lived a block away on Stratford Road; she was a formidable athlete and one of the two or three best students in class, with a perfect- attendance record that eventually covered all eleven years of public school. But my affection, though genuine, may have been influenced by the fact that she had a tennis court of her own.

Mostly—the girls of Miss Wilson's first-grade homeroom apart—I watched the opposite sex at a yearning distance. This romantic *angst* ended with the advent of dancing about

the time my friends and I turned twelve and were forced at
last to consider the possibility of growing up. The ability to
do a box step or a two-step was assumed an essential part of
a young man's social armament, and after that it was understood that one had to learn the waltz and, in time, to conga
and rumba. That meant dancing lessons. Dancing lessons
meant girls.

I did poorly with both. In due course I attended dancing
classes at Miss Dorminy's studio in the scandalous Zinzendorf
Hotel on Main Street, often said to be the domain of
Winston-Salem prostitutes, though in passing through the
lobby to Miss Dorminy's ballroom behind I saw no one I
could identify as a prostitute and would not have known
what to look for anyway. The ballroom was a shabby affair,
battered and stale, but Miss Dorminy held court there every
Saturday morning for years, leading generation after generation of girls and boys to the dancing floor and fate, which for
the boys, at least, was comparable to a trip to the guillotine.
She was very patient as she led you through this step and
that, but she was very firm too; and no attempt to escape her
attention ever, to my knowledge, succeeded. Her method was
to demonstrate a step to the entire class of boys and girls,
then lead each one through it in turn, eventually handing
each over to a member of the opposite sex for practise. I
could hardly have been clumsier and never seemed to get the
hang of it to her satisfaction, but others mastered every new

step at once and were ready, as I never was, for the Big Apple and jitterbugging when they reached remote Winston-Salem. The girls were invariably bigger, though sometimes no more graceful, and trying to move them around Miss Dorminy's floor was a nightmare. I did better at home, where Daddy, as agile as Fred Astaire, tried to give me confidence with his own two-step and fox-trot; but the lesson seemed to leave me as soon as I tried it on a girl.

Dancing classes—and there were others after Miss Dorminy's—led in turn to boy-girl parties, which I found equally humiliating to get through, and then to dances. Winston-Salem had its share of families with attractive daughters for whom their parents entertained large ambitions and the means to launch them on what was, for the time and place, a fairly grand scale. By the time I was thirteen this had reached giddy proportions around Christmas, and it continued that way until, in the early 1940s, all the acceptable boys in town marched off to war.

No doubt the way things were done only duplicated what was happening in prosperous places throughout the well-to-do South. Some weeks before Christmas, the ambitious mothers having cleared their calendars with one another, an engraved invitation arrived announcing that such-and-such a girl would be happy to see me, which I knew to be untrue, at a dance at eight o'clock December the whatever at the For-syth Country Club. For me this was like knowing I faced tooth extraction, but the invitation usually had a kicker: a girl's name added by pen in the lower right-hand corner. This meant I was supposed to call the girl and arrange to take her to the dance; and since, being small and awkward and hopelessly uninteresting, I was being invited simply to swell the crowd of socially acceptable boys, I invariably drew a girl who was known in an earlier time as a "Titanic." It also meant I would have to dance with her all evening, since none of the fleeter-of-foot present would have looked at her twice. This is ungallant, but I can add that all of them turned out to be great beauties a few years later. I seem never to have considered the likelihood that in my klutziness I probably sank faster than any of them. I dreamed often of escape to a desert island, but Mother, like the rest of the mothers in town, knew what was up and kept after me till I made the dreaded telephone call.

The dances themselves were lavish affairs: the club was decorated for the occasion, the girls wore fancy dresses and long gloves as well as the obligatory gardenias the boys had provided, and there was always plenty of punch and food at a serving table at the end of the ballroom. A stag line—to which I aspired, hopelessly until my senior year in high school—guaranteed busy cutting-in on all the belles, though not on the "Titanics"; and a wall of chaperones saw to it from the sidelines that behavior remained impeccable. Alcohol was not served, nor did I ever see it outside the club. The dance ended crisply and absolutely at eleven. Couples were discouraged from lingering in the parking lot, no problem with me.

Christmas dances were a staple of our lives throughout adolescence, and as times bettered toward the end of the '30s they grew larger, grander and more numerous—I remember going to dances on six consecutive evenings one Christmas, then collapsing and sleeping two straight days. But I was sixteen before I had any confidence I could shine alongside such smooth operators as Marvin Ferrell and Buddy Sohmer, both of whom danced so well it took your breath away to watch them.

An allied horror awaited at Salem Academy, whose seasonal dances I began attending at about the same time. "The Academy," as it was always called, was the prep school side of Salem College and Academy, and was actually the original institution; it had its own large building at one end of the college campus, and the girls who attended it—some from Winston-Salem—roomed, boarded and went to class in it, watched at every turn by Miss Elizabeth Zachary, the dean. Miss Zachary was a tall woman of piercing eye who looked to me a lot like Eleanor Roosevelt, and she packed the same sort of authority. She taught, administered, chaperoned and was altogether as formidable as possession of all those duties and skills suggests; and she had a list.

It is a blessing that we lack foreknowledge, for my boyhood would have been ruined had I known what Miss Zachary's list held for my future; and Mother, who was one of her friends, carefully kept the dark secret from me. But at thirteen my innocence was abruptly ended by a telephone call to Mother herself, inviting me to a dance at the Academy on some forthcoming Saturday night. Why hadn't she asked me directly, I wondered. Because she knew perfectly well you'd either make up some excuse or accept and then skip, Mother said. But why me, I wondered. Because she has a list, Mother said. A *list*, I wondered. A list of boys from families she's willing to have to the Academy, Mother said. Do I have to, I wondered. There are no excuses, Mother said, except your unexpected death; now to find you a tuxedo.

Though it cannot be denied that Miss Zachary held an accurate view of Winston-Salem boys and their undoubtedly wicked ways, I wonder still if she knew to what torture she was putting us. Academy girls were said to be snooty. Academy dances were said to be dull. But the worst was the tuxedo. It was mandatory. It was uncomfortable. None of us, at thirteen, had one. But the ritual occasion had a ritual accompaniment. Daddy's tuxedo, by now a bit shiny, could be cut down for me. For weeks his tailor came to the house with parts cut and pinned to take further measurements. At last the reduced but hated garment was ready. I was marched to the Frank Stith store on Fourth Street to acquire a formal shirt—though I was allowed one of the new "soft" shirts, with pleats and a regular collar, instead of hard bosom and wing collar—and the appropriate studs and cuff links. I was ready. I was mad. Everyone I knew was mad too. But our fathers got new tuxedos.

Like most dreaded events dances at the Academy turned out to be a lot less horrible than we expected. The girls, in fact, proved to be attractive, and I promptly fell in love with one of them, Ann Barber from Winston-Salem, for whom I continued to have the vapors, though at a distance, throughout adolescence. Everyone looked nice and smelled nice, and the ballroom was dim and romantic, allowing the illusion that one was a better dancer than one was. Miss Zachary, it seems unnecessary to add, kept close dancing at a minimum. At eleven all the boys were sent home.

As matters turned out, I went to Academy dances for years, still wearing the same cut-down tuxedo. Miss Zachary softened a bit, allowed a few boys on the list of whose social credentials she could not have been entirely satisfied; but she remained the dominant presence at the dances, and among the other obligations of attendance was the duty of dancing with her, which I always did with even greater clumsiness than usual. My foot remained firmly fixed in my mouth: on one occasion, assuring a girl with whom I was circling the floor that I could name the exact moment when Carolina football went bad, and did, she stopped, glared at me and said, "That was the day my father became head coach." Cary Grant would have done better.

22

Lost Graces

Another world of another sort lay a hundred and forty miles north of Winston-Salem in Fincastle, the Virginia village of Mother's family's origins, and it was one of our rituals to go there each summer for a long visit with my maternal grandparents. Fincastle, which dated as an official town to 1772 and may have been a crossroads community as much as half a century older, was one of the earliest American settlements west of the Blue Ridge, whose handsome heights were visible only a few miles away. Its age showed in its many fine houses and in its handsome public buildings, its mellow brick churches and courthouse, all of Classical Revival design; and to children it seemed to exude the air of a calm but cozy past, and a little of ours, since our forebears had been pioneers in its long life.

My grandparents Turner and Annie McDowell lived in a big, handsome house, only a block from Granddaddy's office at the courthouse, that they'd owned since the turn of the century and in which Mother and her brothers had grown up. My grandfather's salary of a few thousand dollars a year as clerk of court and county was modest by today's affluent standards, but in the early decades of the twentieth century it made him one of Fincastle's most prosperous citizens. The house reflected that prosperity. Tall, stately and shaped to an ell running rearward along one side of the lot, it was of brick and frame painted a creamy gray with contrasting shutters of a darker gray, with a two-story central front porch, typical of the so-called "Federal" architecture of the Valley of Virginia, flanked by a railed sitting porch extending alfresco to the corners on either side; at one corner, somewhat incongruously, it also had a Victorian tower, according to legend added by a previous owner from New Orleans who'd also placed wrought-iron ornamentation above the high front windows and doors. A beautiful gray picket fence, indented for a center gate, framed the front yard, and behind the enclosed backyard, invisible from the street, stood a latticed chicken yard, a frame building for storing hams, trunks and abandoned furniture, and a vegetable garden, extending through the block, bisected most of its length by a grape arbor, as well as a woodshed and coalshed and a tiny garage where once a buggy had taken a more gracious ease than did the Ford V-8 occupying it during my boyhood. Together they formed a harmonious compound of a sort that has all but vanished from urban and suburban settings but was then, house and dependencies, commonplace. A high degree of self-sufficiency was the goal, and much of it, or the illusion of it, was attained by families like my grandparents'.

The sense the house gave of limitless space differed dramatically from the suburban compactness of home, and it continued inside. A large Victorian parlor, its waxed floor gleaming, its bric-a-brac glittering, opened on the left of the front-to-back hallway, forbidden to children except on special occasions, and it was matched on the right by the library, which smelled of books, cigar smoke and Granddaddy's bird dogs and was forbidden to no one. Behind it stood the dining room with its sideboard, glassed china cabinets and table long enough to seat a dozen, which it regularly did, followed by a pantry lined with tall cupboards and the kitchen, biggest room of all, which contained both an awesome woodstove and a newer stove fired by kerosene as well as tables and cabinets on every side. Upstairs were four immense bedrooms—

Mother's, above the parlor, boasted a bay window and window seat inside the Victorian tower. A shortcoming was the single bathroom, said to be Fincastle's first, which though huge had been created near the turn of the century from existing space and could be entered only from the outside upstairs porch or by traversing other rooms. The house had, in addition, a long screened sleeping porch in which Anne and I had our beds in summer and enough walk-in closets there and on the porch below to compensate for their lack elsewhere. But its greatest aesthetic glory, gilding the lily, was a cantilevered circular staircase rising by an astonishing spiral from the lower front hall to an upstairs landing so large it held both my grandparents' desks and a chaise longue. It was a reminder of lost graces.

My grandparents were lost graces themselves, representatives of a time and place and way of life only dimly remembered today. Both were products of the period immediately following Appomattox—Granddaddy was born, in fact, only a little more than a year after the surrender—and both were, as a result, fundamentally and permanently affected by the men and events of the war. Because both were the children of Confederate soldiers, and soldiers of the Army of Northern Virginia at that, they seemed to me the very embodiment of an epic age, already part of the Lost Cause and all of the romantic tragedies it summarized, as they seemed to sense. A trio of Currier & Ives lithographs of Robert E. Lee, Stonewall

Jackson and Jefferson Davis hung along the circular staircase, perpetual reminders of a noble struggle, and a larger, grander portrait of Lee, framed in gilt, adorned another wall, pointing the path of duty and self-denial to small boys inclined to easier ways. My grandmother, raised to venerate that legendary past, could remember the Union soldiers of Reconstruction striding Fincastle streets, calling them "bluecoats" in contempt of their harsh, unwelcome presence; she despised "Yankees" with a fine Calvinist zeal, and when two of her three sons, my uncles, took brides from upstate New York, she took to her bed in grief and mortification. Granddaddy, worldlier and wittier, saw the comic irony and chuckled, but he was no less a Confederate loyalist and often told me how his father had walked home on bare feet from a Federal prison in the spring of 1865 across a Virginia parched and prostrate from the wounds of four bitter years. But if Confederate sentiments and delusions of class and chivalry were the foundation of their lives, their household showed little preoccupation with them; until the illness and infirmity of old age finally laid them low theirs was a singularly vivacious family circle. Mother was the last person on earth to harbor a disabling nostalgia, and my uncles, when they were there during my boyhood, were lively young men more interested in sports and girls than in dusty legends.

Mamma—as Anne and I called our grandmother—was a formidable woman who believed in giving her family and guests a perfectly functioning household under any circumstance. Since the place and her family were large and company frequent, she was demanding a lot of herself; but she had help—besides a cook (sometimes two in the summertime, plus Emma to bake bread and serve) she had a black cleaning woman who came weekly to do the heavy work; a black yardman to do the lawn, shrubs and flower beds against the house and fence; a black gardener to tend the vegetables in back and a younger black man, son of the yardman and brother of the cook, to see to the furnace, screens and wintertime stoves, as well as to wax the floors, wash the windows and make spot repairs when they were necessary and possible, though if larger carpentry threatened, Granddaddy being manually helpless, Mr. Dillon, the town carpenter, could be called in as he walked past on his way home for lunch or supper. Mamma wholly trusted no one's competence or judgment, however, and oversaw everything herself. Laundry was taken out several times a week, to be returned, still damp, to the kitchen, where she supervised the ironing by whatever black hands were available. It took a great many black hands, in short, to keep the house running.

That it ran as smoothly as it did owed as much to Mamma's relentless supervision as it did to the hard work and efficiency of the help. She was a perfectionist in an age innocent of racial self-consciousness, and like Mrs. Gerald O'Hara she had no doubt that her exacting standards were as

good for her servants as they were for her family. She saved
her true severity for the latter, moreover, treating her hands
with an affectionate firmness that was noticeably milder and
more patient than what she allowed the men around her, all
of whom she seemed to regard as rowdy, unkempt and in
need of an immediate bath. Toward Mother and Anne, her
only daughter and oldest granddaughter, she showed a gentler
face, as if the three of them, as well as her jolly sister Lila
Godwin, my great-aunt, were a superior gender beleaguered
by barbarous males—and indeed they formed a quiet minor-
ity amidst a conspicuously masculine household in which
football, baseball, basketball, tennis, golf, hunting, fishing,
horses, dogs and smoking were perennial preoccupations. She
seemed to take such matters as inevitable but regrettable,
pursuing her own domestic duties and outside interests in
music, gardening and the architecture of colonial Virginia in
aristocratic disdain for the apparent insensitivity of her father,
husband, three sons, son-in-law and grandson; she was a
Beckley, she seemed to say, and English, and thus above such
roughneck Scotchmen. I remember her as regal and aloof,
with her upswept dark hair and stiff Gibson-girl style; not
unkind but unbending, someone whose disapproval I would
be wise to avoid; and avoid her I did, those long summer
days, on one occasion hiding up a tree across the street at the
Crushes' when she called me.

Granddaddy was different, not only from her but from the
stereotyped grandfathers of advertisements and movies.

Instead of being round, pink and white he was wiry, tan and sandy-haired, and with a temperament wholly unlike Mamma's in its equanimity and good humor. In appearance he was the perfect Scotchman: small, bald, hawk-nosed and spare, trim and precise in his movements in a way that even in his old age suggested the athlete he had been. He was a good horseman and a fine shot, but his local fame was as a skater on the Town Branch pond below Jail Hill, where as a youth he cut figure eights, jumped barrels and regularly won the races across the ice then a familiar town sport; his old skates still hung on the back porch alongside the mounted antlers of a buck he had shot years before. Like many outdoorsmen he'd developed a disposition of patience and calm, but that tendency had been reinforced by his work as county clerk, in his day the central administrative and political position in rural Virginia government; and its typical incumbent occupied it for decades, becoming in the process the repository of insight and wisdom about local families, buildings, places, politics and history as well as the enormous body of truth and legend nowadays called folklore.

But as a boy I only glimpsed this eminence. He was the boon companion of my Virginia summers instead, an unfailing source of information, ideas and amusement who despite the sixty years' difference in our ages talked to me readily, as if I were an adult too, who was always available for conversation or a long walk around Fincastle, of whose residents and buildings he had an encyclopedic knowledge. I do not know where the ladies of the family ate breakfast, or when, but I always took mine with him, the two of us only, he at the head of the long table where he always sat, I at his left elbow where I never sat except then. Being altogether a gentleman of his generation he invariably wore a white suit in the warm weather, linen or Palm Beach with vest and vest-pocket watch to match, and came to table, even the breakfast table, that way. Though finicky and spare in his eating, he seemed to like breakfast food, sausages and fried apples especially with cup after cup of black coffee alongside; and he seemed to enjoy our talks then too, when he often told me the old myths and legends and ghost stories and then fired riddle after riddle to test my wit, though today I remember only one: "Two ducks in front of two ducks; two ducks behind two ducks; two ducks beside two ducks. How many ducks were there?"

Just before nine, however, he arose, bade me good day, took his hat and stick from the table in the hall and set off up the street to the courthouse, generally dragging his cane along the picket fence to make a clackety-clack as he passed. But that was not the end of our mornings together. An hour or so later I picked him up at his office and crossed the street to the post office to await the morning mail. Most of Fincastle went there with us, watching their boxes, already opened, as letters, papers and magazines were sorted out. When the last piece had gone into the last box someone in the rear room shouted, "All up," doors slammed shut again and the crowd spilled onto the sidewalk. The day's dramatic high point over, I got to carry the family mail home.

Granddaddy was a McDowell, hence garrulous, but less so than his sisters and brothers, who had talked corpses into the ground. Gab, geniality and an extraordinary memory for names and faces were essential ingredients of successful politics, in any case, and they were equally valuable in the clerk's office, where he daily encountered demands on his time, energy and diplomacy that went unmentioned in the Virginia Constitution, by which the nuclear positions of rural government, including his, were established. He was often called out at night to issue marriage licenses; county supervisors leaned heavily on his knowledge of land and families; and of course no property transfer occurred in Botetourt County without passing titles and deeds of trust through his vaults, while all wills and probate papers automatically ended there. He had a deputy, his boyhood friend Bob Housman, but the bulk of the work was done by hand and by the two of them alone; the typewriter and primitive adding machine were aids of a sort but nothing more, no secretary assisted them and they transcribed every document in pen and ink; and so they remain most of a century later, a large part of a Virginia county's history in the tidy flawless calligraphy of two men born in the 1860s.

Like everything else I did with Granddaddy I loved going to that office in the near front corner of the courthouse. The Confederate monument stood just beyond the window; the revolving cast-iron courthouse gate was a perennial pleasure; and the steady stream of lawyers through the big bright room, the brass spittoons and the smell of cigar smoke made it a friendly male citadel where everyone else seemed to adore Granddaddy as much as I did. He let me type letters to Daddy and my distant North Carolina friends, and now and then one of the lawyers would take me across the corner to the drugstore for one of Mr. Mayhew's fountain Cokes.

The family grew larger at lunch, after which everyone—almost everyone in Fincastle, it sometimes seemed—napped for an hour or more, and larger still at dinner, when the big table filled and often spilled over. Besides my grandparents and us, the most regular member at table was my great-aunt Lila, by all odds the sunniest person of the family. By the time I remember her she was sixty, white-haired and pigeon-plump in the dowager fashion her generation then favored; but in her day she'd been one of the town's belles, and she was still strikingly handsome, always beautifully made up and stylishly dressed. Younger than Mamma by three years, she was a magnificent contralto who'd studied voice with private teachers at Hollins College, then married Claiborne Godwin, Fincastle's most dashing bachelor, a veteran of the Spanish-American War who represented a textile manufacturer by turns in Charlotte, Spartanburg, South Carolina, and New York, where by World War I they had a large apartment at the West Side Tennis Club in Forest Hills. By my boyhood

Claiborne had died, however, and she, who'd led so sophisticated a life in New York, was back in Fincastle, comfortably
settled in her parents' "Tuscan villa" house on Roanoke Street
a block from my grandparents. She still traveled a lot, dividing the winter months between Winston-Salem and New
York, occasionally taking long trips to Europe with
Claiborne's "Aunt Pidge" Lee, but never in summer, which
she spent faithfully in Fincastle, providing spillover space for
times when visiting family members exceeded the capacity of
my grandparents' house. Anne and I loved to be exiled there
when my cousins paid one of their visits; Lila, never severe
and nowhere near as strict as Mamma, let us stay up late
playing and listening to her resplendent Stromberg-Carlson
radio and kept lavish supplies of candy and cake on hand.

Mother's brothers were at table less regularly by the '30s,
being launched on careers and marriages of their own; but
they were vivacious presences. James, the oldest, was four
years younger than Mother but closely attuned to her. He
was a fine athlete and scholar who, after V.M.I. and service as
an Army lieutenant in 1917-18 had gone to work as a "leaf
man" for the Reynolds company in Greece. He and his wife
and children paid infrequent visits to Fincastle, but his
powerful personality kept me in awe. I was closer to Stuart,
the second of my maternal uncles, who charmed everyone
but awed no one. He was ten years younger than Mother,
thus always a little boy to her; and the air of a little boy clung

to him all his life. Full of high spirits for the larks of youth, he too was a V.M.I. graduate, and the nickname given him there—"Peter," for Peter Pan, the boy who never grew up—clung to him for good. He was an engineer who built roads and bridges and on one memorable Fourth of July when I was seven or eight packed me into his V-8 and drove me to nearby Eagle Rock, where he was supervising the construction of a new bridge across the James River; what he hadn't told me was that they were blasting that day, and when the charges went off across the water I thought they were the finest fireworks I'd ever heard.

Turner, the third of my uncles, was fifteen years younger than Mother, thus by far the baby of the McDowell family; but he had the best balance of the lot. Like James he was a fine athlete and student; but when during his second year at V.M.I. he injured his foot and could no longer march, he had the necessary surgery in Richmond, then blithely transferred to Hampden-Sydney College and had the effrontery, in a family for which V.M.I. was a religion, to say he *preferred* it. Mostly I saw him while he was still in or fresh out of college, and on his infrequent visits home. He was wonderfully good-natured and had a calm, even temperament that made him a more soothing presence than either James or Stuart. He was fun to be with, especially at baseball games, for he had an encyclopedic knowledge of sports and could remember the details of every game he'd seen or played in.

The extended family—though everyone in it would have hooted at so pretentious a term—included Granddaddy's brothers and sisters, Lila's sisters-in-law, who were also Daddy's cousins, and the customary Southern collection of distant relatives and treasured friends connected by marriage, long acquaintance or even—like "Cousin Bud" Carper, who dropped in for dinner one night and kept on coming, without let or surcease but entirely welcome, for the next twenty years—habit so venerable no one could remember its origin. The long table in the dining room was often filled to overflowing on summer evenings, pushing Anne and me to the "children's table," which we loathed, and when our cousins were in residence, onto the porch.

The air at table was invincibly patrician, for the family were keenly conscious of their Beckley, McDowell, Craig, Neville and Kyle forebears, and no bourgeois notions of genteel propriety inhibited their perpetual talk about politics and religion. But none wore their aristocratic trappings more proudly or flamboyantly than Nan Reid and Mary Ed Godwin, Claiborne's sisters and thus great-aunts of sorts to Anne and me. Almost inseparable but clearly distinguishable, they lived at Godwin Cottage, a mid-nineteenth-century house facing Fincastle's immemorial Big Spring from a little hillock screened from vulgar view by weeping willows and immense English boxwood. They'd grown up there, with Claiborne the children of Dr. Isaac Godwin, who delivered half the town and repaired the rest; it was and is a house of singular charm, mellow brick festooned with ivy and creeper and topped by a widow's walk, and its own charm was enriched by that of its two occupants. Mary Ed, the older, was acidic and haughty, with one green eye and one brown, who with her bobbed gray hair and bangs looked like a china doll. Nan, widowed in middle age, portly and jolly, brown hair short, cheeks crimson with rouge, was given to lusty conversation and bawdy jokes. Both used the broad Tidewater "a" for almost everything, though their ancestral pride was in their descent from the Claibornes of Louisiana. They read everything published and held robust opinions about everything done, said, thought, written or intimated, and never hesitated to express their views with energy, sometimes vehemence—especially Mary Ed, who refused to speak to her own sister-in-law for a year beacause of Lila's admiration for the voice of Frank Sinatra. They climbed Main Street to the post office each morning in summer bearing parasols, and after getting their mail and having a Coke at the drugstore unfailingly called upon Lila, even during the Sinatra crisis. Nan served as liaison.

Their black cook was said to serve the best table in town, but the Godwins were often at ours, probably the only place in Fincastle where their gift for contention seemed modest. But Anne and I loved to visit them in the afternoon—though *never* sooner than four, their naps being sacrosanct—when Nan enchanted us, as small children, with a trip to the "circus" made by the nooks and crannies between the shrubs of the huge front yard, ending with the "sideshow" at the old latticed gazebo near the lower corner. Her gift for conjuring the beasts, freaks and clowns was so complete a triumph of inspiration and imagination that I still see them, more than half a century later, when I spy Godwin Cottage. Mary Ed had a magic of her own, after the circus serving us tall, icy glasses of grape juice and ginger ale on the long, narrow back porch. The house, Jeffersonian in its look, was a single floor bisected front to rear by a broad hall onto which all the rooms opened—all, that is, but one, the exception being the little bedroom at the rear, reached by a roofed brick walkway, that had been Claiborne's as a boy and from which, one night in 1898, he'd stolen off to join the cavalry for the war in Cuba.

But—spoiled little city children that we were—we were easily bored during those long summers in Fincastle. Without the variety of amusements Winston-Salem offered we found the time heavy after a week or two of small-town novelty and chafed till Stuart came to take us swimming. Daddy drove up from North Carolina on Friday nights, always bringing presents, and we hung on the fence waiting for his car. Once a week Mamma, Lila and Mother were driven to Roanoke to shop, lunch and have their hair done, taking us along to see the invariable movie at the Grandin before we came home. Anne had friends—Betsy and Kaki Stoner, Patty Painter—

but they had to play in one yard or the other. Boys were luckier, freer: they could roam, and did, and my Fincastle friends—Billy Simmons, Benjy Haden, Allen Painter, Felix Bathelemy—and I had a wider range on which to play our games of hare and hounds, to "hunt" with BB guns, to take an occasional ride across the mountain to swim and fish at Simmons Camp on Craig's Creek. Once Stuart took me to an "air show" at which a dog was parachuted from an autogyro. Once James took us all to the real circus, Ringling Brothers, Barnum and Bailey, where I got autographs from Clyde Beatty and Hoot Gibson, a momentous event.

The Fincastle day reached its climax in the evening, when whatever family was in town assembled for dinner. Granddaddy, the perfect squire, presided from the head of the table, to which leaf after leaf was added as the company mounted. He ate little but urged the rest to ignore him, then spoke so amusingly and at such length no one could. Mamma, at the foot, nearest the kitchen, sniffily inspected every dish brought in, and at a time when dining was hearty and food cheap she had much to examine. Emma, who always came to Virginia to take care of Anne and me, served, sometimes assisted by Elsie Taylor, a black woman with whom Granddaddy kept up a steady comic dialogue. But everyone else talked too, generally all at once, so that the dining room thundered with voices and the clatter of silver and china.

Afterward the entire party moved, in immemorial Southern custom, to the front porch, where the conversation continued to the chirp of crickets and the drone of mosquitoes, and was often joined by this friend or that dropping in from the sidewalk. Drink was neither expected nor offered, and the passerby left when he'd said or heard enough. Mosquitoes came to stay, however, and the duty fell to Anne and me to fetch the gun from the hall and spray the ladies' ankles with Flit. Sitting and talking on the porch at night was a central social occasion, generally continuing until eleven or even midnight. Sometimes, egged on by Granddaddy or the porch-sitters at the Crushes' across the street, I played my harmonica. Some nights the town band rehearsed creakily in a lodge hall up the hill. But mostly people talked until the small hours, though Anne and I were sent to bed on the sleeping porch upstairs long before the last tale was told. Through a window opening onto the curving staircase I often listened as long as I could keep awake, occasionally glimpsing the glow of Granddaddy's cigar while overhearing what I realized years later was the mythology of Virginia: who was kin to whom, who'd married whom, who'd disgraced which family, above all the endless story of the Civil War . . . the matter of the South as surely as the Arthurian legend is "the matter of Britain," and the dubious legacy, haunting but inescapable, of every Southern boy of my generation.

23

In the Hills

The other great ritual of my boyhood summers was camp. Most of us went most of our summers between early boyhood and early adolescence, and a few went on after that, as junior counselors or even counselors. But all of us did not go to the same camp. Committed Scouts went to Camp Lasater. The rich boys—never really part of our crowd anyway, though they sometimes joined us for football or baseball—went to the expensive camps of western North Carolina, Camp Sequoia and Camp Black Bear, in the mountains around Asheville, camps with their own uniforms and horses and perfect lakes ringed picturesquely by pine forests, camps that kept them most of the summer; and even some of the older boys I knew of more modest means, sensibly exploiting friendships made at Davidson, Duke and Carolina, turned up there too as counselors or instructors. A few rich boys went to similar camps in Tennessee or Georgia, camps as expensive for eight summer weeks as a year at prep school, and a couple were sent to dude ranches in Colorado and Wyoming. The rest of us made do at Camp Hanes.

Summer camp was a rite of passage; and in later years I have come to realize that, for all their cosmetic distinctions, not to mention the gaps between them in cost, the camps we went to, North or South, Christian or Jewish, fancy or plain, actually were far more alike than they were different. As grown men looking back we recalled landscapes, atmospheres, experiences and even people of an almost eerie similarity: Camp Hanes, Camp Lasater, Camp Sequoia, Camp Black Bear, Camp Maxwelton, Camp Arrowhead, Camp Gemstone, Camp Hiawatha—they were all the same.

Both Winston-Salem camps attested to the generosity of Winston-Salem millionaires. Camp Lasater bore the name of a pioneer Reynolds vice-president, and its acreage and facilities were projections of his interest, curious in the father of three daughters, in the Boy Scouts. Camp Hanes took the name of John Wesley Hanes, one of the city's early textile men and the father of several of its most prominent citizens; but it was the "Y" camp, owned and operated by the Winston-Salem YMCA, and that reflected a Hanes interest too, though no Hanes son or grandson spent a summer at Camp Hanes. Their summers were spent at the palatial places their families kept at Roaring Gap, an enclave of the wealthy in the Blue Ridge Mountains northwest of the city, or at the expensive camps near Asheville.

This is not to suggest that they had skimped on Camp Hanes, however. Unlike Camp Lasater, which remained rough, perhaps as a deliberate challenge to ambitious Boy Scouts, Camp Hanes was tailored and elaborate, even elegant for what was intended, after all, to familiarize boys with the out-of-doors; and besides being comfortable and fastidiously maintained, it was constantly being improved and enlarged, so that by the late 1930s its construction and amenities rivaled those of the finest boys' camps in the country. Winston-Salem millionaires were not niggardly philanthropists, and at Camp Hanes everything from waterfront to tennis courts, from kayaks to crafts pavilion, and from mess hall to rifle range, was as good as the best.

Camp Hanes was an extension of the Winston-Salem "Y," for which the city's well-to-do also provided handsomely. Located on Spruce Street half a block off Fourth Street in a sturdy modern brick building put up in the 1920s to replace an outmoded predecessor, the "Y" stood at the heart of downtown, readily accessible to business and professional men who liked to swim or play handball or volleyball at lunch and to small boys willing to do either or all whenever they could. The pool lay at a lower level from the lobbies, which carefully separated the men from the boys, with the gymnasium and track above it and handball and squash courts, which were also used for fencing, still another half-story up; and boys could reach neither locker room nor gymnasium and pool until a desk clerk pushed the button that opened an electrical lock to the doorway giving onto the stairs, though on the men's side access was easier. Almost all of us were enrolled in "Y" gym and swimming classes from the age of seven or eight, which gave us fine indoor athletic facilities throughout the year, and many of us learned to swim and run relays and lift weights and shoot baskets there on scheduled afternoons or Saturday mornings. Separate swimming and gym periods were reserved for what were then called the "underprivileged," whose memberships were subsidized by the "Y" and its angels and of whom, in those Depression years, there were aplenty needing both "Y" and help. The building served, moreover, as an inexpensive residential hotel for town bachelors; and the boys' side sponsored a number of neighborhood clubs for grammar-school boys, called "Gra-Y," as well as a single, community-wide "Hi-Y" into which we all eventually blended upon entering high school. The unsurprising result was that, like the Boy Scouts, the YMCA—to which, evidently without discomfort, all of my Jewish friends belonged—was a central part of our lives as boys, so that going to the "Y" camp was like moving from one part of the building to another.

Its site lay just above twenty miles northwest of Winston-Salem at the foot of White Wall, one of the four Sauratown Mountains. Pilot Mountain, a famous North Carolina landmark because of its lonely eminence and odd camel's hump, stood by itself eight or nine miles west of camp, White Wall rose directly behind it and Moore's Knob and Cook's Wall, both of them higher and rockier, lay a few miles due east; together they gave campers alpine heights to challenge and the area, otherwise little more than rolling pine woods punctuated by scrubby farms and tobacco barns, what little topographical distinction it could claim. A large ell-shaped artificial lake, dammed at the outside of the bend and perpetually replenished with clear, cold spring water, made a rough peninsula of the central part of camp, with two rows of five board-and-batten cabins, each descending the slope to the water on either side, and the stone headquarters building, where the director and his family also had a small apartment, at the upper central point where they arced together. The mess hall, a larger stone building, stood perhaps a hundred feet across grassy, open ground behind headquarters, its back to the mountain, and the tennis courts and ball field lay on higher ground to its rear, with a single, rutted, country road running past them to be split, a little further on, into a series of trails leading to the top. Additional buildings went up during my camp years—a large, open, stone pavilion that served as a crafts shop, a separate infirmary, eventually a new cluster of cabins to house younger campers—but the original symmetrical design remained, with a few off-center adornments to give its neatness and orderliness interest.

My first season as a camper, 1934, probably would also have proved my last had it not been for the camp's policy of offering enrollment in four ten-day periods, so that a boy could take as many as forty days or as few as ten; for my initiation I had taken only the first period, and it nearly turned out to be more than I could handle. Then hardly beyond its first decade, Camp Hanes was still roughly finished and even more roughly run. Its director, "Skipper" Long, was the "Y" athletic director, a bald, barrel-chested man who looked like a football coach and acted like one: a kind man, to be sure, but a believer in learning by the harsh test of experience, which in my case meant, simply, sink or swim. No serious swimming instruction was offered and the only limit on the use of the lake was that swimming could be done only during specific periods of the day. No part of the lake, which was large, deep and had a long shoreline full of hidden coves, was off limits, and no "buddy system" was enforced. Since I still did not swim—was, in fact, somewhat afraid of the water—and since Skipper Long's vigorous doctrine insisted that one hit the water at every legitimate opportunity, I spent ten days in terror, egged on constantly by him but sinking like a rock whenever I got beyond wading depth. Adding to my misery were the facts that I was the youngest boy in camp, by an uncomfortable margin the smallest, and that it rained heavily every day. I was not wholly inept. I learned to row both flat-bottom and tin-bottomed boats and caught a few fish, and I played ball for the cabin with great gusto. But I remember camp that year, when I was nine, as dark and my spirits as gloomy, and only the jolliness of my counselor—Edmund Schwarze, a senior at Moravian College preparing for the ministry—and the good will of Lawson Withers, Brooks Bynum and Henry Stokes, older Winston-Salem boys serving as counselors, kept me there. Fear, perpetual damp and the certainty that I was in over my head, often literally, combined to make me powerfully homesick.

By the time I was ready to try again two years later everything had changed. Skipper Long had been replaced, as athletic and camp director, by Douglas Grimes, who though inevitably called "Skipper" too had a gentler, wiser way with boys still feeling themselves into a strange new environment. A large but carefully defined section of the lake had been reserved for swimming, and a new swimming pier, lifeguarding team and buddy system had replaced the rugged but dangerous waterfront discipline—or indiscipline—of an earlier day. Grady was going, which helped. But the most important consideration was that I was older and bigger—only two years older, to be sure, and not much bigger, but by the crucial inch and pound that made the difference. I signed on for three periods, a month, and drummed my fingers till the big day arrived.

When the chartered Greyhound bus had passed out of sight, returning campers whose time had expired to the downtown "Y" from which we'd set out an hour earlier, Grady and I found ourselves in the competent charge of Wiley Fleenor, a recent graduate of King College who had Arch Taylor, an older friend whose father was mine's closest crony, as his junior counselor. The rest of Wiley's cabin, a tough-looking bunch from Statesville and Salisbury, settled in with us.

Each square little cabin had its own front porch, a clean-up area marked by a single faucet on the lower outside wall, where we hung our metal basins, and four sets of double-decker bunks inside; an extra cot or two was brought in if a period proved oversubscribed. Campers "policed" their cabins for inspection daily; and the organization of camp life revolved, in fact, around the individual cabins, their members and, most importantly, their counselors.

In the latter respect I was immensely lucky every year. Not everyone always was: counselors came, like eggs, in a range of grades, and it was mostly random fortune that gave one camper a successful counselor, another a mediocrity. But from the first, otherwise a flop, I was blessed with sensible, wholesome young men, most from nearby colleges or medical schools, who not only understood boys and were patient with them but—what camp directors everywhere must pray for— fine models of honorable male behavior. Edmund Schwarze my first year and Wiley Fleenor my second were followed by Lawrence Reid, who after Davidson went on to become head of Washington Mills; John Lawrence, a Wake Forest man who became a noted Baptist minister; and, my last year, my lifelong friend and virtual older brother Charles Speas, who followed M.I.T. with a successful career as an international engineer. Other counselors who lent Camp Hanes character and warmth were Charlie Welfare, for my generation the perennial embodiment of the place; his Statesville friend and Wake Forest classmate Dent Weatherman, who looked like an Indian and swam with the grace of Johnny Weissmuller; Roscoe Wall, who lived on Buena Vista Road and was going bald at twenty; and Bill Speas, from my second family, who served several years as camp doctor while in medical school and, like the others, was to become a North Carolina practi- tioner. What perhaps should be noted in a more cynical age is that their high human virtues did not make them or their colleagues sanctimonious stuffed shirts and that I never, then or later, heard a whisper of scandal about them and their ser- vice at a boys' camp. In both senses of the word it was an age of innocence.

The camp day followed vaguely military lines, with a flag-raising ceremony at sunup and bugle calls throughout the day to announce meals or to mark activity periods—riflery, archery, crafts, boating, tennis, baseball, swimming; one arranged one's day according to a schedule worked out the first day of camp, and an experienced camper, which by the end of my second year I had become, learned which hours in which activities suited him best. All campers were required to swim at the two swimming periods, morning and afternoon, and to take instruction in the "bull pen" until qualified to paddle the wider waters of the main aquatic area; with the help of Charlie Welfare and Dent Weatherman I gradually overcame the fear of water Skipper Long's rough tutelage had left me and "swam the lake"—crossed its two-hundred-foot width on my own, though carefully accompanied by Roscoe Wall— and entered the privileged circle of real swimmers, discovering all at once that I could do the breaststoke, butterfly and backstroke as well as the crawl as soon as I gained the confidence the water demanded. I loved boating too and then canoeing and kayaking, both of which required special tests, among them the ability to right an overturned vessel and reenter it from the water. On the range I improved my marksmanship with the .22 Winchester rifle Daddy had given me and taught me to use, and I qualified up to Sharpshooter. Crafts and nature study amused me less, but I did enough of both to pass the tests; and I played tennis daily, boxed in the tournament and teamed with Grady, he pitching, to make a formidable battery for Charles Speas's cabin. At the evening campfire I played harmonica in the "jug band" and listened with undiminished horror to Skipper Grimes's ghost stories, which by my last year I could have told, without missing a syllable, myself.

Eventually camp palled. By 1939 I was fourteen and had acquired part of a paper route, developed an interest in chemistry and discovered girls, none of which I could pursue from the rural wilds of the Sauratown Mountains. More to the point—though less clear to me then—after five years I had done nearly everything camp offered, usually often: I had swum every stroke, rowed every inch of the lake and fished every cove and eddy of its periphery, played and sung every campfire song and heard or told every joke. I was not so much jaded as numbed by the familiarity of every detail; I had at last, quite literally, outgrown Camp Hanes.

Of one recurrent activity I never tired, however. At least once every summer a special day was set aside for hikes to and up the surrounding mountains. Groups of counselors led each party—you had to choose which peak to try—and trucks brought out a hikers' lunch to break the march, which for all but White Wall was considerable; but we climbed the rocks hand-over-hand for ourselves, and at Cook's Wall descended through a series of limestone crevasses, covered with lichen, called with romantic gusto Tories' Den. By my last year I had scaled them all and knew the trails and hidden clearings of each, though my favorite remained Moore's Knob, from whose craggy eminence I once glimpsed the skyline of Winston-Salem gleaming like a silvery Oz twenty miles eastward in the plain below.

24

Finalities

What I was too innocent to realize until years afterward was that the summer of 1939 was the end of many things, boyhood among them. As the '30s neared a close, my grandparents aged visibly and our trips to Fincastle grew briefer. In July 1939 Granddaddy died during my last month of camp, and Mother began the hard task of closing the big old house and bringing Mamma, by then too sick to live there alone, to Winston-Salem. The last week of August I set off, with three dozen other boys, on a trip to New York and the World's Fair at Flushing Meadows arranged by Skipper

Grimes. It was the first time most of us had traveled so far, let alone to New York, and we celebrated our new freedom and maturity—I was fourteen, like most—by smoking cheap cigarettes in our rooms at the Sloane House "Y" on 34th Street and trying to worm ourselves into the girlie shows on the Midway. The fair, in turn, celebrated "The World of Tomorrow" with spectacular exhibits imagining a future of multilevel cities set in the center of huge, fertile plains tilled by happy farmers. We loved it; loved seeing Gary Cooper, escorting a pair of what movies and advertising had taught us to call "statuesque" blondes; loved the Aquacade and its stars, Johnny Weissmuller and Eleanor Holm; loved the parachute drop; loved the Bronx Zoo and the "El" and seeing a television displayed at Radio City Music Hall; loved attending a radio broadcast of a concert by Bob Crosby and the Bobcats sponsored by our own Camel cigarettes. Afterward, sick from smoking and hot dogs and staying up half the night, we climbed glumly back into our chartered Greyhound bus to come home. It was September 3. In Washington we stopped at a corner just past the White House to let Skipper Grimes buy a copy of the extra newsboys were crying the length of Pennsylvania Avenue. Hitler had invaded Poland. World War II had begun. We understood that, but not that before it was over we'd all serve, and some die, in it. Nor could we guess that the sweet, safe, innocent America of our birth and boyhood soon would vanish, as boyhood would vanish, forever.

A NOTE ON THE TYPE

The text of this book was set in Perpetua, a typestyle designed in 1932 by Eric Gill, a British artist and book illustrator. Its small and compactly fitted letters give it a clean and engraved air.

Composed by Superior Typesetters, Inc.

Printed and bound by
R.R. Donnelley & Sons Company
Harrisonburg, Virginia

Book design by
DEBRA L. HAMPTON